ENLIGHTENED
LIVING

by
Martin Faulks

TITLES BY MARTIN FAULKS

www.martinfaulks.com

Becoming the Lotus (2009).

The Path of the Ninja - An Englishman's quest to master the secrets of Japan's invisible assassins (2015).

The Emerald Tablet - A Commentary on The True Path of an Adept (2015).

Shugendo - The Way of the Mountain Monks (in conjunction with Shokai Koshikidake) (2016).

Future Publications

Hermetic Meditation.

Enlightened Living

By
Martin Faulks

Falcon Books Publishing
2017 Second Edition

2017 Second Edition Published by

Falcon Books Publishing
www.falconbookspublishing.com
Second Printing: 2017

ISBN-13: 978-986-94925-1-5

FOREWORD

Often with spirituality today, there is an apparent disconnection between spiritual practice and the awareness of actions in daily life. This misunderstanding can often cause a hindrance to the practitioner in their development and the practitioner is often left wondering why they are not progressing. *Enlightened Living*, offers a solution to this current circumstance in a practical and easy to follow guide.

This book addresses the many obstacles that we may face in life that often hold us back from moving forward. Keys are offered to enable integration and harmonization, using the value of our meditation practice to fuel and perfect our daily life. These keys include examples such as, dealing with negative thoughts, repetitive cycles and developing discipline in a meditation practice.

Martin offers clear and effective keys to overcome these obstacles and highlights the importance of a spiritual practice along with awareness throughout our daily life. By combining these two aspects in a harmonious way, success is guaranteed in both the inner and outer life.

As Martin illustrates,

'Only when our knowledge of inner technologies and abilities matches our outer progress will we reach our full potential.'

Those who have already read and applied these principles laid out in this book have purported its life changing effects. For this reason, an extended version has been produced to offer further guidance, clarity and inspiration to those seeking harmony in every aspect of their life.

This book it is both refreshing and life giving in its delivery and application. It is indeed a treasure for those seeking an inner wealth, to conquer life's outer challenges and offers the tools to ride the chariot of success in every aspect of life.

~Tanya Robinson
Owner
Falcon Books Publishing

DEDICATION

To humanity in all its colours.

ACKNOWLEDGEMENTS

Thank you to Kindra Elizabeth Jones whose tireless editing brought clarity and focus to this work.

With special thanks to Tanya Robinson for transcribing the original talks.

Make Every Action Reflect Your Inner

Nature

TABLE OF CONTENTS

INTRODUCTION

When you first start applying the principles outlined in this work, you may begin to notice a change to your normal waking consciousness. One of the first things most people observe is greater control over their thoughts. Often people just starting out also describe a heightened sense of self awareness, and notice that they are more able to focus on tasks and complete them with calmness and efficiency. Some students even note that others around them have remarked on how much they have changed. As you continue, you will start to amplify this positive effect and this will begin to stabilise. You will find that you will start to operate at a higher level of functioning. This is a very powerful method, so get ready for a big change in how you interact with the world. This will not only be in relation to your sense of self, but also how others view you.

Up until this point there may have been many areas of life that you have naturally avoided, or made excuses for not achieving your best in. Perhaps you have decided that a certain skill is not important, or that it is beneath you to perform. Often you can see that people who have a strong skill set in one particular area of expertise, will often devalue others who possess a different skill set in another direction. For example, scholarly people sometimes see practical skills as base, in contrast strong practical people sometimes see those in academia as disengaged and weak. As soon as you start to really engage you need to be honest with yourself. You need to let go of your existing limited sense of self based on your current skills and start to expand who you are. Often changing how you see yourself is enough to discover you are quite talented at something that you have previously been avoiding.

Think back to school and the group of children who seemed to play football every lunchtime. Despite them practicing day after day, year after year, they never seemed to really improve. It seems unbelievable doesn't it? Imagine practicing a skill an hour a day for ten years; I would expect my skill level to have improved greatly, no matter how hard the skill. This situation, no matter how strange it may sound, is the norm.

Have you ever noticed how many things people attempt to do without really trying? They may ask directions, but then do not make any effort to memorise the advice they are given. Perhaps you have noticed some people who constantly lose the same objects, or make the same mistakes with no sign of learning. Everyone has a friend that complains about the same problem, but makes no effort to change what they are doing in the situation and continues to deploy the same strategy. So why are we not improving the things we practice repeatedly?

The truth is unless we make an effort to improve, our ability at any one task will remain the same. We have a tendency to progress to the level that is required to avoid discomfort and then stay at that same point. Only when we do something with the intent to learn, with an effort to do our best, will improvement be our result.

Please take a moment to imagine what your life would be like, if from this moment on you fully engaged with all tasks. Picture what would happen if you really tried to improve every undertaking you are a part of. Every day you would improve on all levels, with unbelievable results. Visualise what would happen if whenever you needed to use your memory in a task, no matter how mundane, you made a real effort. Just think of the knock on effect in other areas of your life, how your memory would begin to improve on a daily basis and what long term effects this could really have.

Now imagine this across all areas of your life. What if every time you communicated with someone you really tried your best to communicate as effectively as possible? Using the right words, tone, timing and method to achieve the best possible outcome. This would lead to you being more efficient, maybe instead of several emails going back and forth the first would be enough? The extra time this would free up would allow you to put your focus into other areas, continually improving.

Likewise, if every time you wrote your signature you treated it like a calligraphy class, when you placed your glass on the table you did it with precision and care, or every step you took was executed with full calm awareness. Soon every movement and action becomes a practice on balanced coordination and ability. From outside it would seem as though you are naturally talented at all sports, all physical undertakings or activity. Your mind and focus would become honed and perfected with every waking moment.

Take a few moments to imagine if this principle spread like a light throughout your whole being, covering all aspects of life. If when you rested, you really took time to relax and recover, when you imagined you really pictured things and when you made love you really did so with all your heart, fully engaging with every moment with the whole of your being.

Have you ever heard the saying, 'the whole is greater than the sum of its parts'? If so, you may be able to picture how each and every improvement can have a knock on effect on everything else, resulting in improvements far greater than you may at first believe are possible. From this moment onwards make a silent vow to yourself that you will make the best effort towards every single thing you do. Do not put anything beyond you or beneath you. Every action you take will be done with full wakefulness and direction. You will know when reach this exact state when a sense of wholesome joy forms. When you get dressed in the morning do it to the best of your ability, when you exercise, study, work, tidy, etc. really aim to improve. Apply this to all aspects of your life, from every mouthful you eat to every word or action. Once this is a habit suddenly everything becomes easier.

This practice is a sunlamp on your soul and will speed your progress in in a way no other method can. Really focus on the areas you have previously found hard, but be aware humans have various mechanisms to avoid things we find tough. We may make excuses and tell ourselves 'I am not that kind of person', or look at some tasks with disdain, maybe due to fear of failure. This is a form of avoidance. Perhaps, we are holding onto some outdated negative beliefs or fears. These modes of thinking can often prevent us from making the changes we need to move forward in our daily life. Often a big change in attitude or sense of self is needed. There are times we need to let go of past events, opinions and even overcome the doubts and prejudices of others. Errors are an important part of learning and should be embraced as such.

As you start to embrace all aspects of your life as chances to express your higher self, your personality starts to balance. Many inner barriers and shortcomings start to become healed and transformed, as you become increasingly on target with your actions, a clear vision of what you are doing in life and how the world works naturally forms.

As you progress the small changes that you make in your life will start to have a harmonising effect on the world around you. You will find the best way to do things in the most integrated way. This book is a guide which contains insights for those who wish to follow this path I have just outlined. A set of life adjustments passed on from those who have gone before us and who have fully applied themselves to this process. But why should you dedicate yourself to this path?

The most important moment in your life is this very moment.

Enlightened living is the art of fully embracing the present. Your life is now, right here in this very breath. Each and every word and action you make are permanent, they cannot be erased and their ripples echo for eternity.

This is very important.

There are no rehearsals for life.

No way of repeating a moment or of trying again, so we need to do our very best in every second of our time here. We make this dedication not for ourselves, but for all living creatures. It is our way of saying thank you for the greatest gift of all, that of being alive.

This book is all about this joyful undertaking, it is about being the person you want to be now.

Many of us dream of healing the world of its problems through our positivity. Perhaps part of us is aware that we are not separate, but rather sparks of consciousness in the big picture of existence, the effects we have on those around us during every moment of our being should not be underestimated. For decades the human race has been dreaming of a new way of being, of living in harmony and peace with everything around us. In our hearts we know that as a race we have been sent here on Earth as caretakers in order to bring a utopian balance to the planet. Great teachers have appeared throughout our history who have woken up to the big picture and utilised various methods to implore the human race at large to do so too.

If we look at the ideals and dreams underlying our various spiritual teachings across the globe you will see a common thread, a common set of goals. The great master of Christianity proclaimed,

'By the fruits you will know the tree.'

And Hermes Trismegistus is said to have uttered the immortal phrase,

'As above, so below.'

It is time for the human race to make the change it has been dreaming of for so long. It is not enough for us to pray, meditate and resonate with high ideals in our studies. We need to apply these lessons to our lives too - to make our words our prayers, our thoughts our meditation, and our actions reflect our ideals. It is time for us to be in harmonious awareness in every moment. It is time for those who study spiritual disciplines to step forward and show the qualities they espouse in a very real and material sense. To grasp and bestow the power of these fundamental ancient teachings, and most importantly to implement them. If those of virtue who seek peace and kindness do not take the reins and direct our race, then who will remain in control?

As you read these words the human race is ripping the world apart, digging up every fossil fuel, fishing, hunting and killing whole species of animals to extinction and destroying forests like an unstoppable fire. To power this machine, the populace are working to exhaustion for the promise of power and status in the form of money. The moment a baby is born into the modern world, they become a part of a world that encourages, if not forces, competition. This is not a useful method to aid us in a life like that described previously and can lead to short-term and short-sighted decisions of what is so often perceived as a 'successful life'.

To what end?

The start of a better approach is to be found in yourself. To make this happen you need to start by making an ongoing beautiful program of self-improvement. To do this you need to learn to be aware, to correct your mind, to change your ideals, to cultivate goodness, to remove all barriers to learning, and to raise your consciousness. Then with enlightenment, you can live a life of excellence on all levels. Excellence is not achieved by competing with or domination of others, but through being in harmony and at one with everything.

HOW TO USE THIS BOOK

This book consists of a series of contemplations, lessons and insights, each designed to aid you in the process described in the last section. Sometimes they contain important principles concerning aspects of life, good health, or insights into the nature of the mind. Often in this text you will find suggestions of different ways of thinking, correcting your mind or methods of taking advantage of how your mind already works. Of course, all of these principles can be applied on many different levels.

It is suggested you work through each section contemplating the lesson it contains and, if inspired by it, spend a month or so applying that lesson or change to your life until it becomes habit. As you progress you will find you are starting to become more aware and possess a more engaged mind state in your daily life with increasing ease. Those who practice meditation are of course undertaking a dedicated training program in which they sit in the ideal state of consciousness which we are seeking. These people will find the lessons in this book far easier when applied to daily life.

With each insight and adjustment of the mind comes great reward. However, the reader may also find valuable lessons in the areas that they disagree with the author over, as much as they find in those that they agree with. We all need to find the way that is most suitable for us as individuals, this is simply a guide to what I have found works.

Whenever a change in consciousness happens and stabilises, an improvement is seen throughout life. Once this change has occurred, it is then time to move on to the next lesson, using each section as a means to amplify this dedication to living fully in every moment.

WHY THIS BOOK IS NEEDED

If you visit any library or bookshop throughout the world you will find the shelves full of manuals outlining techniques of meditation and spiritual improvement. Techniques handed down through generations of practitioners, from mouth to ear that are designed to train, improve and sharpen mental abilities.

In the distant past, these techniques were viewed as a means of training our consciousness for everyday life. The practitioner would use their practice time to sit in meditation and to create the qualities that would allow them to reach their full potential in daily life. These vibrations created in the consciousness would naturally pass over into their everyday thinking. The practitioner would consciously apply the skills gained whilst training and carefully assess which techniques were working, then make the necessary changes to their practice based on their everyday interaction with the world. Their goal was to create a constant state of mind that was imbued with awareness, compassion, dedicated purpose and ability to learn. This ongoing sense of improvement came to be known as 'enlightenment'.

In a world with so much confusion, where people naturally drift from their goals and are pulled around by their emotions, someone who had gained the ability to keep a clear focus stood out. They were able to stay on target in every moment. This person was truly connected with the world in a harmonious way and in every action expressed their highest potential. To the enlightened person, every moment was a moment of joyous improvement.

As time passed the idea of enlightenment changed and became distanced from the present. Dreams of a lofty position beyond strife evolved as practitioners wanted themselves to reach a point beyond illness, beyond hardship and most of all beyond effort. Everyday life became secondary to the practice itself. Practitioners focused on improving their meditation skills and cut out other aspects of life in order to focus better on these arts, rather than practicing meditation in order to master life.

So it is that a peculiar reversal has occurred, where the training methods have become the goal. This could be seen as a form of confusion and present in many aspects of human life. Unfortunately, this has led to a great inversion of these qualities regarding spirituality. In real life, the application of the skills and abilities gained in meditation are no longer assessed. Techniques that are ineffective, or that were designed for a very specific purpose, are passed on thoughtlessly and have been applied without any sense of direction or goal. Ineffective training has become the norm and techniques are chosen because of their 'colour' or how enjoyable the method is, rather than for their original intended purpose.

The modern spiritual seeker finds himself in a very difficult position, surrounded by authorities with great titles and magnificent clothing telling him to be humble. In some cases, taught by practitioners who are unable to cope with the normal world and hide away, never facing and overcoming the very challenges that they hope to guide their students through. This state of hypocrisy we are facing today is prevalent within spiritual communities, where the mastery of the real challenges which are associated with a life of being human are concerns of the future that will be cured rather than being addressed now. This book hopes to be part of a revolution which addresses this imbalance - responsibility is firmly placed back in the hands of the individual once again.

The teaching methods used to achieve this are wisdom, focus and higher consciousness in everyday life. So that once again we can create a result based practice. Once again, practitioners will be associated with stability, practicality, clear vision, and, above all, excellence through harmonious action. True enlightenment cannot be hidden because it shines forth in every thought, word and action and creates goodness wherever it touches. This book is to aid readers in applying these enlightened principles to their daily life.

Here is an interesting test to see how awake you are. You can try on yourself and on the people you know. It is a test to see how awake you really are. Next time you visit a friend stand in their garden and ask them how long have they lived there for. The longer they have been there the more impressive this tends to be. Then ask them to point to the North. Most people will find this very hard.

They will respond with a sense of confusion enquiring, how do they tell which way is North or how would they know that? The truth is, ever since they have lived there a giant fireball has been careening across the sky from East to West every single day, and they must have been asleep not to have noticed it. Ask them again where the sun rises from to point out the direction and most people will be unable to do so. How is it possible to live somewhere without noticing something this big and dramatic happening every day?

CHAPTER: 1

Discovering The Point In Life

Why are we Here?

This is probably one of the most profound and searching questions that a person will ask themselves at some point in their life. So often we find ourselves looking to find the point of life. There comes a time in our evolution where that question becomes less of a mystery as we begin to gain a deeper understanding of our purpose here.

We can draw upon the metaphor of a particular television show to illustrate the point. This television show was a competition in which a team of competitors were led into a series of different rooms, and each room contained an exciting new challenge that they had to overcome. They were not given any instructions, but had to deduce what the challenge was by the contents of the room. Contestants would view objects in their relationship to one another and within their context to enable them work out the given challenge. For example, maybe they were led into a room that contained a very high ceiling, on which was hanging a crystal from a thread. As they looked around they would see there were two ladders and a length of rope. Through deduction they would conclude that the mission was to obtain the crystal and the objects were there to aid them in this.

The contestants may be inclined to use the rope to lasso the crystal, or somehow to balance on these two ladders to reach it. After some experimentation and contemplation, they would find the best approach was to get the two ladders and tie them together to make one long ladder. They would all work together to hold the ladder in the middle of the room, while the most agile and lightest team member would climb up the ladder and retrieve the crystal.

Now, life is a bit like this game. We all start without any memory of where we come from, there are no clear instructions as to why we are here, or what we should do. But, as we grow so does our awareness and we get a chance to deduce by our self-knowledge and by exploring the world around us what we are going to do with our life.

The first thing we tend to discover is our own body. Then we meet people who love and look after us and the beauty of existence slowly unfolds before us.

As we get older, we discover some interesting things about this physical vessel that we inhabit. We discover it is subject to injury and that we can become ill. From these experiences we learn that one the first rules in life is that we need to take action to try to stop these negative things from happening and we need to keep this body healthy. We also learn to be more aware and thoughtful, and by understanding more about the world around us, we can do this with increasing efficiency.

By looking at ourselves we discover some interesting things. Our physical body has some areas that we can control. We can tense our muscles, we can control our voice, and we can focus our senses. However, there are other areas that are outside our control. For example, our heart and organs are a part of the autonomic system nervous system which allows them to operate independently from our conscious control. We are also able to observe there are some aspects of life that occur without any form of direction or involvement.

The same is true of our mind, we have some instincts that respond automatically to danger and are free from conscious control. For example, if we accidentally touch something which is very hot, our natural reaction is to withdraw quickly without even having to command it.

We also have strong recommendations from some parts of our mind that are outside of our

3

control in the form of emotions. This emotional warning system, or recommendation system, is very accurate. It tells us how we should respond to every circumstance we encounter and even prepares our body for the required reaction. We are aware of the flight or fight responses within the body. When we experience fear, the body responds in preparation to flee from danger, our heart rate will increase and we may sense a state of anxiety. Also, if we experience excitement, the body prepares itself ready for action. We do however, discover fairly early on that this system is a little out-dated.

Although the emotional responses are there to protect and assist us in recommending the best course of action, sometimes these responses appear to be somewhat primeval in their approach. For example, if we are working on a computer and we experience frustration with a functioning problem, often the response is to react negatively, becoming angry and sometimes even wanting to use violence. Well, smashing it perhaps worked at an earlier stage in evolution, but the smashing it solution is not so useful now and in fact would cause more problems, not less.

So we discover there are aspects of our mind that need to be managed carefully in order to have the best possible outcomes. We also discover that sometimes these emotions can interfere with our perception of things. So they need to be paid attention to, but we cannot let them control our decisions.

Later on, we discover that this body ages and that all living things are subject to death. We also find out that there is a time limit to this life, this means that we had better value the time we have here. It means we cannot repeat the time that has passed and every action is very important. For this reason, we should do our best to be who we want to be and have the effect we want to have now. It also means that for very long-term projects, those that exceed the span of a single human life, we need to work together as a team. I think this a very important lesson also.

When we look at the outside world we can see that we belong to the animal kingdom. We are made of the same material, we have the same needs and wants, and we feel a great affinity towards animals and do not like to see them injured or harmed in any way. Within the animal kingdom there is a naturally established hierarchy, this is especially evident among pack animals who have different methods of competing. To establish dominance in their pack they will bark, roar, display, or fight. Look around and you will see this same behaviour expressed by our race, albeit in a different manner.

We still do a bit of all of those things, but for the most part we have moved to a new mode of operation whereby we use money as a status and power indicator within our pack. So important has money become, that the whole of our society is based upon it. As we speak people are burning down whole rain forests, destroying whole species of animals, shooting and hurting each other, cheating people, and doing anything they can to gain a higher ranking within this pack order.

Deep down we know that this is not what we are here for. If we observe most spiritual philosophies, this soon becomes apparent. We can compare various religious traditions and can see that these similar ideas and ideals are expressed. Likewise, in fictional writings and films, our race expresses its dreams of Utopia, of Atlantis, of the Garden of Eden, to name but a few examples. This is the goal that lies within ourselves, an expression of our true calling.

It is clear that we, the human race, are not here just to compete and gain physical possessions. Indeed, in our hearts we are all in agreement of what we are truly trying to do here. It is this leftover, instinctual mechanism that needs to be directed carefully to create the best outcomes. Because we are in control, we have a responsibility.

We know we are the caretakers of the world. We know we are meant to be looking after this place. We know we are here to create an environment in which all manner of life can thrive, interact with each other positively and to learn more about existence and evolve.

So the inner goal reflects the outer goal; we want to cultivate health, harmony and tranquility in ourselves and the world around us.

We know that our consciousness is meant to be evolving, which naturally happened when we were young. It is also clear that we should be preventing negative things from happening to our own bodies and to other people.

So, just like the Hermetic principle 'as above, so below', our inner and outer worlds reflect.

Within ourselves it is easy to see that we should be standing for and cultivating health. On the bigger scale, just like with our bodies, we know that the world is subject to harm and illness.

We know we should try our best in every moment and be fully aware because we have a limited time. And because we die, we know we need to work together if we want to have a good long-term outcome.

When we look at our inward intentions, we want them to match up with our outward actions. So we want to keep our intentions pure and actions skillful.

Likewise, we want our consciousness to continue evolving and have an inbuilt desire to keep learning about the world around us.

You can see by our fiction, when we are exploring space, we have dreams of our future technologies.

So far we have established why we are here, so that is very good. There have been various wonderful spiritual teachers who have helped us wake up to these ideas, to stop us from blindly fighting and hurting each other for material possessions.

It is my belief we are ready for the next step, which is to manifest these good intentions here and now. To do this we need to start looking for results on all levels because these confused tendencies tend to redirect us.

This is evident even in spiritual traditions. There are some cases within spiritual communities whereby the focus of an individual, or a group of people, has been redirected from a genuine desire to serve, towards seeking power, money, or pleasure. They may even go to extremes in their outward display due to confused purposes.

Because of these tendencies within the human condition, it is necessary to make sure that we are looking for balanced, harmonious and integrated development. It is therefore important to embody the changes we want to see.

This not a new mission, this is your responsibility. You were born in charge of everything that is you. You accepted that mission the moment you took your first breath. You said, 'I am.'

So what are you going to stand for?

In order to make sure we do not go off track the key word is harmony. Without looking for harmony on all levels, it is easy to become selfish again, to stockpile or get more of. People can compete on all levels. They can compete on more of anything. They can compete on who is more compassionate, who has renounced the most. So we look to be in harmony with all things.

So we start with good intentions, our good intentions are to have the best possible outcome for everyone. Once we start off with those good intentions then:

1. We intellectually develop our mind and keep our mind healthy.

2. We use our mind to prevent negative things from happening.

3. We use our mind to make sure there are good outcomes. We develop our emotions and our creativity.

4. We use our emotions in such a way, as to have clear vision intellectually, we are also working logically to see things clearly and understand what the world is trying to communicate to us.

5. We listen to what the emotions are saying and make sure they are an accurate reflection of what is going on.

6. We help that emotional mechanism to update itself.

7. With our physical body we make sure everything is in harmony, balanced and healthy

8. We do our best to make sure that our words and our actions reflect these noble intentions.

Each spiritual system has evolved to have balance, whether it is perceived through the chakras or sephiroth, or the dealing with the elements. We inherently know if we go into one area too much, this will develop into an imbalance and will present itself to us in one form or another.

Another aspect of our personality which is worth noting, there may also be a tendency to start to cheat. So, instead of trying to achieve things the right way, we devise an approximation that involves the intended goal, once again either walking on someone else or competing for something in an aggressive or hurtful way. So it is important for us to be fully integrated. Once we have embodied this goal, because we have been looking for harmony, we have now created around us the very reflection of who we are.

Although we are in this world, we are not of this world. In the sense of, we need to make money, but we are going to do so with the aim of empowering everyone and with the awareness that there is enough for everyone. We are not going to fight or do anything wrong for it, or with the intention of causing any harm to anyone or things to obtain it. If we all do this we all start to embody the change we are looking for. Then a ripple effect occurs, and a change in vibration happens. In this sense, the collective consciousness of our race is like that of a young child just waking up to itself and the effects of its actions.

There is only one question left now, since we have established what the point in life is and we all know why we are born here.

How much are you willing to grasp it?

CHAPTER: 2

What is Enlightenment?

There are almost as many definitions of enlightenment as there are people talking about it. I would like you to join me in a meditation to create a clear understanding, a vivid picture of what it would be like to be enlightened and what that goal exactly means. Furthermore, what would it be like to meet someone who had obtained it?

Our minds tend to work better initially with negatives because we are hardwired by evolution to see threats. So, to begin with I would like you to imagine the opposite of enlightenment, a scenario of a person's life where nothing is working for them. Let us contemplate someone called John.

John has a back injury which is extremely painful, he finds himself hunched up in positions which are very uncomfortable and very negative for his the rest of his body. This causes other problems and leads to further pain. He cannot exercise very well, his appetite is poor and for this reason he does not eat very well. He takes pain killers to cover up that pain and this causes him to find it very difficult to focus at work. The worse the pain becomes, the more frustrated he gets with life, consequently the more drugs he takes.

Eventually, he starts taking illegal drugs to supplement what he has been prescribed and loses his job because of it.

We can imagine how confused this poor man is by now. He does not know who his friends are and often thinks that people are being unkind, vengeful, or wish to cause him harm. He finds himself moving into a circle of friends who also help to supply him with this temporary relief, however this is the complete opposite of the companionship he needs to help him improve his life.

We can imagine this man eventually being hard to approach because he is very confused with what is going on and his emotions are in the wrong place. By now he barely eats at all. The toll of this and the drugs impacts on his appearance and makes him unapproachable. You can imagine how easily he could end up in a mental hospital and at the lowest ebb that a human can reach.

So here we have imagined the opposite of someone who has achieved enlightenment. If we look at John's life we can see that there is no learning going on, his diet is wrong, his body is wrong, his mind is wrong, the people around him are not working and everything is out of place. In short, nothing he is doing is effective in his life. His very spirit could even be affected, so that he exudes negativity and hatred. In his perception the whole world has failed him and you can imagine if you met this John, his negativity could easily pass on to you.

Now we are going to think of the opposite scenario. This time imagine a situation where everything is working. We could term this aeonic consciousness, enlightenment, adept-hood, whatever you want to call it. It is the pinnacle of spiritual attainment which is referring to the premise of everything working and in harmony.

Let's turn our attention back to John, but this time we will view his life as becoming enlightened.

In this scenario he begins to learn meditation. Initially it is very hard for him. His body is in the wrong position, so he has to learn to focus on his breathing and improve his posture. At first, he can only meditate for five to ten minutes a day. Over time he improves his practice to a twice daily routine of twenty minutes. He finds just those two twenty minute sessions of meditation a day are enough for his posture to begin to change, and also his mental attitude. He not only notices less back pain, but there is also less mental pain and he begins to become calmer.

Have you ever noticed in life that things tend to have a knock on effect?

If one thing goes wrong, then you notice something else becomes affected, that affects another aspect of life and so on. Let us return to John. Now, because he is in less pain, he is able to reduce his medication, so much so his mind starts to become clearer. As he continues to practice his communication becomes more harmonious. As his emotions start to become more balanced and his judgement improves, he begins to make better choices and he also starts to correct his mistakes. His diet improves, giving his body and brain the right nutrients, therefore the correct glucose levels are maintained at all times of the day, also helping to keep his emotions stable. His breathing becomes regular, deep and calm. So his whole body is fuelled correctly. You can see how if this cycle of improvement continues, John could get close to what some would view as enlightenment.

Viewing the world more clearly, John now sees opportunities where before he would miss them. So now he has changed his job to one that allows him to really thrive and his routines of exercising mind and body have helped him to manage his life without medication at all. All the solutions are inside of him. Having stabilised his life, he can now turn his attention to perfecting the different areas of his life. Now he is calm and aware, and steadily everything he does continues

16

to improve and is able to live fully in the moment. Now, we are getting very close to a vision of enlightenment.

Let us take it to the next step. Imagine a fully enlightened person who is always engaged with what they are doing and everything is always working harmoniously. Imagine everything starts to get close to its ideal, optimum state. For example, they have the ideal team around them, they have the ideal attitude, they are adaptable, aware, and they are fully awake, always learning. Their body is perfectly positioned, their breathing is good. They are eating correctly. Due to the combination of all of these things, they make something stronger than the sum of its parts and this is what we call enlightenment or adept-hood.

CHAPTER: 3
The Stages of Enlightenment Attained Through Meditation

Almost every spiritual tradition worldwide has its own form of meditation practice offering various approaches and methods. Some get the practitioner to focus on specific words, such as repetition of a symbolic phrase or mantra. Others instead focus on an image, or playing a musical instrument.

There are some practices that involve keeping a specific image in the mind's eye, or focusing on a painting on the wall. Some very beautiful schools keep the mind on the breath, or on a specific part of the body. Some use posture, sitting in positions conducive to the meditative state. There are even traditions that use walking, or a repeated movement as a focus to aid them in creating an inner calm. What all these schools have in common is that they are practicing a form of concentration that is designed to lead them into a meditative state. Meditation, however is not concentration alone, but rather a state of being that can be achieved by the practice of concentration.

The ancient Indian masters used to call meditation *Samyama*, which translates as the ultimate self-control. This can be classified by the following elements:

Earth

The first state of meditation focus is that of concentration and corresponds to the element of earth. The Indian yogis call this state *Dharana;* in the West we talk of contemplation. Whilst in this state we learn to make our focus rest on one point by holding it there with a firm, unmovable intent. Our mind becomes as solid as a rock and as stable as a mountain. We are imperturbable and hold our subject in focus through sustained concentration, whereby the attention continues to hold or repeat the same object. To master this ability we need to overcome all major disturbances or traumas in our personality and develop a balanced and healthy lifestyle.

Water

In the second level of attainment, which corresponds to water, the mind finds itself naturally drawn to the subject of meditation. This is known as *Dhyana* to the yogis.

In this state our consciousness naturally works with us, and no longer needs forceful fixation on the meditation subject. Our mind is still focused on the object of meditation, but, as our skill improves, we develop the ability to make our thoughts naturally drawn towards the subject of meditation. Our mind is like a river, gently and constantly flowing towards the object or area of meditation naturally. By staying self-aware and not forgetting ourselves, we maintain the stream in the direction we require and the subject of meditation becomes like a magnet, pulling our thoughts towards it.

Our active role becomes to simply protect the flow from disturbances. This is the most commonly achieved state of *Samyama,* so much so that it has come to characterise meditation. Indeed the term *Dhyana* is often translated as meditation and is where terms such as *Zen* and *Chan* come from.

To master this art we must eliminate any conflicts or negativity in our being and direct our whole life towards good outcomes.

Air

In the third state our mind, like air, becomes so close to the object of meditation that it takes on its form. This is known in yoga as *Samadhi* or union.

In this state of deep absorption only the essence of the object, place, or point shines forth in the mind, as if the mind were devoid even of its own form. Just as air is invisible yet still present, so the self totally disappears during this stage. In this state we fully experience the object of meditation so much so that, just as the light from the object travels through the air to the eye, there is often a state of confusion between the object of meditation and the meditator themselves.

This state is often accompanied by a feeling of bliss with amazing insights. To master this state, we need to master our own inner desires and to resolve any issues we have with the path of life, fate and death. We need to be able to detach and let go of all worldly things at will and bring all aspects of our personality under control.

Fire

In the Hermetic tradition this final stage is known as 'Becoming Aeon', the yogis call this *Nirhija Samadhi*, and relates to the fire element.

In this state our consciousness is like a radiating heat, comparable to the rays of the sun shining forth. Now we can become whatever we choose, just like heat becomes at one with any object it touches. To truly grasp this it's important to understand that heat is not separate to the object, but is in fact part of the object it is within. In this state we no longer have any confusion between the self and subject, only the subject exists. Rather than beings that are meditating, we are becoming the task or becoming the subject of meditation, unhindered by any obstruction.

To master this stage of development, we must let go of all confusions and our perceived limitations. We must defeat vice and ignorance to embrace our true nature.

CHAPTER: 4

Learning to Tell the Real from the Apparent

The first step on the path to enlightenment is being able to tell the real from the apparent.

A bird with a nest in a tree believes it owns that tree and in particular its perch. If a rival bird arrives it will make a lot of noise and chase it away, protecting what it believes to be its territory. In the same way, humans often believe that by exchanging money they gain the right to an area of land and control it. There is no difference, no one really owns anything.

The truth is a lot of the things we perceive as real are just human constructs - titles, qualifications, class. They are not real things because they do not change who the person is. They are simply just objects and labels which we, as a society, use by agreement.

We have a limited time on this planet and most of us spend our time pushing objects backwards and forwards to each other. A bit like in a game of cards, in the end everything goes back in the deck - no matter how tightly you grasp it.

The same ideology can be observed with money. Money is a made-up concept, printed to exercise control and make sure that we work by dividing the power amongst society. It doesn't matter whether you are a lord, a policeman, or a rock star, the reality is that you are still just a person. Your true virtue is how you treat others. That is your real value, there is no title or rank for that.

As a race we place worth on objects, yet in reality nothing actually has an inherent value. A diamond and a pebble are both just stones, yet we have decided we prefer one more than another. A piece of rag and a piece of silk could have the same insulation qualities, so have identical usefulness as a top, we just prefer one over the other. But the actual object does not have an inherent value, it has a usefulness under specific circumstances. The amount of water in a puddle is valueless if there is an abundance of rain, however the same amount of water in the Sahara desert would be considered priceless due to its lack of abundance in that location. We believe objects to have an inherent worth, but that is also a human illusion.

This is the real world here.

CHAPTER: 5
The Greatest Barrier to Enlightenment

It is a shared goal across many cultures to strive for a higher state of being, either through spiritual achievement or enlightenment. I believe the greatest barrier to this goal is in fact the idea that this state is separate and distant, beyond the reach of most practitioners. Usually it is thought that by practicing a particular technique, gaining secret knowledge, enacting a special initiation, or following a set of lessons, you or I could be promoted and transformed into a completely different person. A person beyond shortcomings, who doesn't make mistakes, only has the purest thoughts, and is able to answer any question. To me, this is unrealistic and, by being so, places it firmly in the future and allows us to excuse ourselves from exercising our full potential in the present.

On a lower level, we find this kind of thinking reflected in those who procrastinate when making the changes they want in their lives. It is always going to be tomorrow or next week, rather than now.

Enlightenment is in the now, and if you undertake an action with good intentions, thus meaning you are looking for the best outcome for everyone and in everything, with pure awareness, then in that moment you are enlightened. You will find when these two qualities are combined that it bring with it all the other attributes that we would associate with enlightenment such as being in harmony, always learning, and with a clear idea of what you are doing.

So the idea is to make this state of consciousness our normal functioning state of consciousness. To do this, it is very important to learn to fully engage in what is happening right now. To always remember that the enlightened person is not going to be beyond troubles, but is rather someone who skilfully deals to the best of his or her ability, with the goal to bring about the best possible outcome. So when a negative thought enters the mind, it is corrected and then transformed into something positive. Rather than assuming failure at the presence of a negative thought, it is important to correct the mind. It is unrealistic to expect to never have those kinds of thoughts. Indeed to me this very act of transforming a negative action or thought into something that has positive intentions and outcomes embodies the highest expression of enlightenment.

There are techniques that can help you with this goal. Meditation is a wonderful one because you actually practice the very state of mind that we are discussing here. When you meditate you are practicing being enlightened, you are practicing that state of higher consciousness. This makes it easier to bring this mind state into your everyday life. There are other techniques to wake you up and remind you to be doing what you are meant to be doing. So some traditions use prayers at regular intervals, some use affirmations. For me, I like using inspiring statements, for example the Zen saying:

'I will respectfully advise those who wish to be enlightened, do not waste a moment of your life.'

Many people hear this and think it means to work really hard, but in reality it means to fully engage with whatever activity you are doing. So if you are having fun, then really have fun. If you want to go to sleep, really go to sleep. If you are working, really work. Do not waste your time and effort by not being fully awake or engaged. In this way I find I am able to be far more efficient than many people and fit more into my day, since energy is not wasted through split focus.

> *'Every moment is an opportunity to be enlightened.'*

This quote is often interpreted in one of two ways. The first interpretation is that of a sudden breakthrough, some form of great epiphany or realisation that will bring around accession to a new, enlightened state. The second interpretation is one more based on expressing our own inherent enlightenment. Every moment is an opportunity to be enlightened, therefore to embody our highest potential in each action.

The next quote is also from the Zen tradition and encapsulates the simplicity of their teachings. Often the previous statement is difficult to apply across all areas of life, and it may be that you find yourself willing to accept second best for some aspects, putting the responsibility of accepting your full potential into the future. Whenever I catch myself doing this I ask myself:

> *'If not now, when?'*

This quote is a poignant reminder and allows us to fully engage and create perfection in the present, rather than a distant goal. It makes us reevaluate what we find important and prevents procrastination, allowing us to fully engage with all aspects of life now. A useful exercise is to imagine how what we are doing could be done perfectly now, not how we could improve on it in the future but rather in this very moment. A western quote, which I believe is adapted from a sentence in the Hermetic literature and perfectly describes this is as follows:

'Life is too short not to be exactly who you want to be. Therefore make sure each action embodies who you really are in this life.'

Following on in the same vein, a personal motto of mine:

'Make every word and action reflect your true nature.'

This statement is a wonderful reminder to stay on target, as it helps us to be aware of our own behaviour and focus on good intentions.

Affirmations like these are aids, but, like many techniques, unless they are tested and applied in daily life, they are but mere trinkets and their value never realised. The same can be viewed regarding the analogy of an athlete who is a sprinter, but whose focus is on training rather than practicing his sport.

The importance of applying these skills in our waking day cannot be emphasised enough. In spiritual traditions this is endemic. As people continually search for new techniques upon new techniques, but never realising that these techniques are only the training, it is the embodiment of the skills, insights and abilities that aid us in daily life.

To review

1. Do not put this off.

2. It will not suddenly happen.

3. Spiritual exercises are training, the true test is applying the lessons to life.

4. Embody the state you wish to happen.

5. Own every single action.

By applying these principles, balance will be found within ourselves because by practicing things that are difficult we become stronger in those areas we are weakest. This acts as a sunlamp on the soul. Skills are transferable, so as we become accomplished in one particular skill, our ability improves in other areas also.

For me, this is the true way of enlightenment.

CHAPTER: 6
Recognising Spiritual Truth

When discerning spiritual truth there are four principles that need to be examined. These are namely feeling, usefulness, knowledge or information, and purpose.

The First Principle of Feeling:
Is this genuine perception?

Genuine spiritual experience has a specific feel/awareness which cannot be reproduced by the imagination. For example, let's say you have a strong inclination that someone is going to visit you on a particular day. A good way to test if this is a genuine sense or not is to then use your imagination to reproduce the same inkling about something you know to not be true. By imagining the same person doing something that is not true and comparing the two, you can test the first. Genuine spiritual insight will have a sense of clarity and honesty, a specific ring of truth and a brightness that cannot be reproduced by your imagination.

When doing this, it is important to use the same sense that the insight came in to test it. For example, if you have a strong feeling, test that feeling against a different one in your imagination. If you see a picture in your mind's eye of a specific image or information, imagine a different type of information in your mind's eye and compare the two. You will find when it is a genuine insight it will appear far brighter, far clearer and have a specific feel to it. After a few months of practicing you will be able to distinguish the imaginings that are produced by your own fears or hopes from those that are from a genuine insights.

The Second Principle of Usefulness:
Will this really work?

Once you have received new information, or a new insight about the nature of how your mind works, or indeed about how the underlying principle of the universe works, then test it.

To do this imagine yourself as an alchemist in your laboratory. Be detached, do not let self-doubt get in the way of any promising results, but also do not let the attachment to the joy of this insight get in the way of discarding it if it does not work either. Use this state to apply your new insight to various situations and examine how effective it is.

This is when you discover whether your insight, which sounds good, is good.

It is important to do this not just to test if it is true, but also to benefit from insights that are genuine. This process of testing and applying will make sure that it is embodied and applied so it becomes a new way of functioning. This is because it's not just important to know how something works, but to employ that knowledge practically. To utilise the insight.

The Third Principle of Knowledge and Information:
Does it match up?

There is a tendency within spiritual communities to lack dedication to empirical investigation of teachings or insights. This is mainly because information has been received from another source, which is often viewed as beyond scrutiny. However, it is important to apply the same rigours when investigating spiritual truth, as we would if we were applying it to any other knowledge we receive. We should not make an exception just because it has been received from a different source.

Indeed one should be more careful with such information, since we are receiving information from the mind to the mind. With every new insight, compare it with research and the insights of others to verify the information. It is important to remain emotionally detached, both to not be too close and not to become too critical either.

In the past I have received specific, valuable information, but after investigation, found that information to be different from historical accounts or that the current research seems to contradict it, and have thus dismissed it. I then doubted the information, but years later found it to be correct. It is important to be very strict with regards to testing our insights, but with practice we can develop clear sense of when we should trust our spiritual senses, especially if they work..

The Fourth Principle of Purpose:
Why is this information being received?

Sometimes we will find our interests take us down a particular line of investigation. It is important to ask ourselves firstly, for what reason are we receiving this information, and secondly, for what purpose are we researching this subject? If after this you find that what you are really getting from it is some form of emotional stimulation, such as approval from others, then it is time to question the motives behind this course of action. Moreover, if the primary purpose does not aid you with your own evolution or helping others, it may not be as genuine as you might think and you need to investigate further.

Now with these principles, if you have learned to apply them correctly, you will be able to naturally look to the stars whilst keeping your feet firmly on the ground. These principles can also be applied to other sources of spiritual information, for example a book. Let us use this to examine how all four principles can be applied.

To begin with we use our senses or intuition to feel if the book is right. You have probably noticed when you read certain books, somehow they feel alive. For me, the sense of how it makes me feel often reflects the wisdom of the book and, when reading such information that is genuine and speaks of truth, you will find it is also significant to your life. The resonance of such words tend to have a balancing effect on your emotional state and it is this kind of literature that we are looking to gain nourishment from. It is possible to test these techniques to see if they work. You can do this by comparing the information you receive with other authorities and other people's experiences. It is good to observe and explore the reasons why you investigating this particular subject. Often the 'why' may just be exploring, but it is important to have clarity in your reasoning. Otherwise, it could be the case where time consuming studies are undertaken which may not be of any benefit to you.

These four principles can also be applied to people. For example, when listening to a spiritual teacher, again be aware of the feel of what they are saying, this can be compared to falsehood in your imagination. It is possible for you to test them directly with a falsehood, you could ask them a question such as, 'I sensed guru that you healed me last night, is that true?' If they reply, 'Yes, I definitely did that,' then maybe their discernment is not to be trusted.

It is also possible to test out and observe their level of ability and technique to see if they are capable of doing what they say they can do. It is a useful practice to do since it is an indication of what skills you will be able to obtain from that particular teacher.

Are their students getting the same results?

It has often been said that we now live in the Age of Information and it is easy to see why. So much knowledge is accessible in the world due to the internet and, with less hurdles to publishing ideas, we have so many more 'experts' offering their services too. Unfortunately, in many cases the evidence points to the contrary and they have yet to achieve the very results they are advertising you can gain by following them. One example of this are the very popular schemes that purport to make money without much work. In fact, under scrutiny most people in the system are not making money, and those at the top who may be, are usually more reliant on those desperate people signing up at the bottom than whatever they claim is making them the money. This same model, with a lack of expertise at the top supported by the emotions of those below, is evident within many spiritual communities.

There are many people who claim to have great knowledge or amazing past lives when they were very competent and special people, but do not show any qualities being associated with either being able to apply that knowledge, or possessing any of these abilities from that past life to the now. Of course you can test what they say against other people's research and of trusted texts within that tradition, but if they are unable to apply it to their own life, then how are they going to help you to apply it to yours?

It is also important to question why certain information has been given to you. If this information does not have a direct relationship to assisting you in some way. Ask yourself these three questions:

1. Why has this information been given to me?

2. For what purpose am I being told this information?

3. Who does this information benefit?

It is important to question the motives of these actions. Often there are very exciting insights and very important things which are told to students, however it becomes a part of an exciting play, where everyone feels a lot better since it enhances their status. It is important to look at the 'why', and if the 'why' is strongly motivated by a financial motive then maybe the validity of information is to be brought into question.

By applying these principles on all levels we gain the ability to be completely genuine. This is important because it is necessary to have spiritual clarity, honour and truth above all things.

CHAPTER: 7

Is Celibacy Needed to Make Spiritual Progress?

This chapter addresses whether it is necessary to be celibate in order to make spiritual progress.

In some spiritual traditions, such as the Taoist and Tantric disciplines, there are specific methods of sexual practices employed to prevent loss of energy during intimacy. It is important to know that the sexual act does indeed use up energy and effort, and there is an exchange of energy. This is natural and in some other systems, the act of stopping this would be seen as creating a blockage in the process.

However, if you feel you do not have enough energy to do your practice or to achieve your goal, in my opinion the first and foremost thing you should look at is not your love life. Instead, look at where in other areas of your life this energy is being used and look to reclaim energy that is wasted in negative actions and emotions instead. Emotions such as anger or jealousy, bad habits or getting into arguments with other people are very emotionally draining and use up a lot of energy. It is these areas we would gain the most benefit from working on first.

It is true that there are some very specific spiritual practices that require minimal energy interference from outside influences, or from forces that the practitioner may not understand or be able to control. These can involve following a vegetarian diet, removing oneself to a carefully controlled environment, or avoiding interactions with people that have a strong energy vibration, whether low or high. But as a general rule, unless you are looking for a monastic life, such extreme measures are not needed.

So first of all make sure you are resting properly, you are eating well and redirecting those negative qualities that absorb energy. This can be physical - anything from a habit with drugs, to relying on a stimulant such as coffee, or being around the wrong people. But can also be due to unbalanced emotions such as anger, worry, or anxiety. This creates blockages within the body's energy system, which in turn uses up a lot of energy also.

All these negative qualities really do take up far more energy than the act of lovemaking ever could. If you feel very tired, an emergency measure could be to become celibate. These practices may have merit in very distinct systems and circumstances, but for those of us wishing 'to be in the world but not of it', we must learn to balance our lives, not create a bigger imbalance.

CHAPTER: 8

Would I Make Better Spiritual Progress in an Ashram or Monastery?

Students who find themselves struggling to make the progress they wish often ask whether they would advance quicker in a spiritual community, such as a monastery or ashram. At first glance, the obvious answer would be 'yes'.

If you decided to enter such a place you would be given a teacher who is from an established lineage and there would also be senior students who are more advanced than you to assist. Often just being around others who have achieved what you find difficult can inspire and help to lift you up. Likewise, you may find being in such a positive and controlled environment also means you can be more scientific, since cause and effect are far easier to recognise. Indeed with less chance of chaotic or uncontrolled events to affect you, you could even isolate different aspects of practice to test them independently. The main drawback to this kind of living would be that without the challenges of everyday life it is hard to see practical improvements in your character, or whether the progress you are making is applicable to the outside world.

The problems encountered with moving into a monastery, ashram or any other circumstance where you are retreating to focus on your spiritual work, depends upon the timing. In most circumstances the ideal time would be when you have mastered the mundane world.

If we imagine someone whose life is like the following:

They have mastered their job and therefore work is easy and enjoyable to them.

They are surrounded by people who are inspired and well-adjusted, they are having a very good life. These people we would consider to be graduates of the school of life.

They have learned the lessons that life has to offer them and, for this reason, they are ready to go to university.

For this person to join an ashram or a spiritual school of some kind would be the ideal choice, since they have learned to master the life given to them and are ready to progress further.

Perhaps in another circumstance the option of living in an ashram would not be so beneficial. Let us imagine someone whose life is rather different:

For them the world is tough, and they cannot cope with some areas of life. Maybe they are unable to keep a job, or their job overwhelms them and impedes on their life.

They find interaction with people difficult. They may have surrounded themselves with people who are a negative influence, or be the negative influence on those around them.

For them it is possible their spirituality is a place where they can get away from the difficulties of life and, for this reason, they think retiring to an ashram is a great idea. They think it is going to be place where they can get away from their troubles and focus on what they find important. In fact what is most important for their spirituality is for them to learn to build the basics before they work on more advanced skills.

So, as you can see, this can be another form of escape and running away from dealing with some of the necessary challenges in life. The very fact these challenges are given far less importance in the person's mind, is an indication they are rejecting the valuable life lessons that they are being presented with. It is evident this person has aspects of their personality that need improvement, development, or in some way to grow up and be transformed. However, if they decided to move to a retreat centre or monastery, one of two things may happen - both of which tend to be negative.

The first situation that may occur if a life lesson has not been fully realised or overcome, is the same challenge reappearing under different circumstances. For example, if a person who dislikes adhering to authority decides to join a monastery or convent in an attempt to escape this, the same lesson may be presented in a different manner. Perhaps even the person assigned to teach them will be just like the employer they walked away from, with the same personality traits they found difficult, only this time they cannot get a break to go home.

Another example of the way this type of situation may arise would be someone who has been following a spiritual route through yoga and now decides to live in an ashram. Their decision may have been led by their difficulty to cope with the workload in their job and they are looking to find rest and relaxation. However, once there they realise that now they must adhere to a strict discipline of yoga and ashram work, which they no longer enjoy as they did when it was an escape. What they were finding difficult before has simply transferred, and now they view the yoga routine as work.

Often in attempting to avoid these lessons we try to change them by changing the situation, but only to find we are only moving from one circumstance to another one. This may come as a disappointment to us and initially quite hard to deal with.

The second circumstance the practitioner may find themselves in if they attempt to avoid the challenges and hardships of life will have dire consequences, for they may actually find what they are looking for! If this happens they will find themselves in a community of others like them, in an environment that does not offer the challenges they need, and then they really are in trouble. For this is when their progress will become stunted and they will miss the biggest opportunities to develop further.

But even in this circumstance, if the teacher is genuine then they will know that there needs to be some fairly drastic changes to bring the person back into balance. The reason being, no learning is taking place, because in this environment the individual will only end up practicing the things they are good at, not transforming the aspects that they have yet to gain skill over. The consequence and danger of indulging in this avoidance, is that the personality will become more imbalanced. This action will only pose a greater challenge in the future, since balance will eventually need to be restored.

It is important to note that if a teacher has set up an environment to also avoid life lessons and hide, then they are not a genuine master because they are not attempting to evolve themselves. If a situation like this occurs, then the environment you are in becomes a prison, not a school, and can only lead to trouble for both the master and student. In that circumstance an individual will not develop at all. They may go through all the motions that appear to be spiritual, but evolution only happens by learning new skills, developing these skills and qualities, and then embodying them.

In various spiritual traditions, all systems refer to the same aspects of evolution, be it the chakras, elements, or the sephirot. In order for the evolutionary process to develop, it is necessary that all areas of mastery need to be covered. Under the circumstance previously mentioned, the worst possible outcome a person who is wishing to evolve can do, is to put themselves in a position where life is easy, where there are no challenges. The consequence being, to live a very one sided life without having to change or improve.

CHAPTER: 9
Does God Punish You?

We have all read accounts of a supernatural being of one form or another punishing an individual or a group for some wrongdoing.

Sometimes this transcends lifetimes and people feel that the divine is punishing them for sins committed in their past lives. A person may even feel that a supreme being actually hates them for these past actions.

I have always felt that these accounts of fire and brimstone are in fact based on simple human misunderstanding. Let us use an analogy to view this idea from a different angle. If we were building a wall, but had got the calculations wrong, a well-meaning outsider may try to warn us that the wall will fail and we need to start again. Unable to see our own mistake, we shun his advice and continue to build the wall. As we continue the wall becomes unsteady, and worried about the danger we are in the outsider once again tries to warn us that the wall will not work. This time his persistence is interpreted as a threat and we continue, determined to not be redirected. Inevitably the wall finally falls down and a brick hits our foot. It is easy to see how this could be misinterpreted as a malicious act on the part of the outsider, his threat manifest rather than our own incompetence and failure to listen to advice.

Likewise, we have probably all seen people in life who have inner demons that control their actions. We may observe that if someone carries a lot of anger, they will often find themselves in conflict with everyone around them. However, if you try to talk to them about it, they have no awareness they are causing the problems and may also interpret your comment as an attack. They see the problem as caused by other people, who are seen to be irritating or causing trouble.

You may have even met someone who has a constant feeling of a lack in their life. They never seem to have enough money, affection or time. They are so convinced that this is the way life is, they create the very thing they fear. So whenever they get money they spend it quickly, because they fear that there is not enough money to go around. In turn they put so much pressure on their friends and demand so much attention, that their friends eventually become tired, or hide away from them because they cannot meet the demands of that person. This causes the person to feel rejected by their friends because of this and in turn to draw on their remaining friends even more. It is a very common mistake to think the causes of our problems come from the outside world, when actually they usually stem from our own inner perceptions.

In the case of those who feel concerned about their past transgressions. It is important they forgive their own mistakes, and make a readjustment to their behaviour first, to create positive outcomes in the present and future. By taking this course of action those who feel punished, will find that their feelings will disappear and be replaced by a positive and healthy outlook on life.

CHAPTER: 10
Mastering the Emotions

Our emotions are important signals never to be ignored. We can imagine them like advisers in a royal court. If you imagine yourself as the king or queen in your castle and each one of your emotions has a different advisory role within the court.

Anger

Could be likened to a war minister who advises on what threats we must eliminate, defend against or deal with.

Sadness

Could be in charge of memorials and of things we need to pay our respects to. Could also help us to be aware of aspects of our lives that are important to us and we would miss if they were to go too.

Fear

Could be the minister of protection, informing us of danger and risks to our health and those around us. A kind of health and safety report on life.

Jealousy

Could be the minister of equality, helping to ensure that we are treated fairly in relation to others. Jealousy also reminds us of what we find important and how to spend our resources.

So as you can see, our emotions are important and we need to learn to listen to them. However, they should have the same position in our mind as I have just described in the royal court. Each emotion is there to offer advice and advice only, it should never take the throne. Therefore no one emotion should ever be in control, but each one should always be listened to.

Likewise, it is important to learn to understand your own emotions. Only when you take the time to listen and understand your emotions will you know which ones are to be trusted and which emotions are often incorrect or overreact. That way it is possible to learn to interact with them in a very healthy way.

If you have a persistent emotion that will not fade or disappear, often this is because we have yet to solve the problem it is warning us about. The result of this is often that the emotion, in an attempt to be heard, starts to shout louder, maybe even seizing the throne. So if these emotions are not addressed in the appropriate manner, rather than deal with them, often we employ all sorts of strange methods to get rid of them. People may resort to taking pills, as a way of suppressing the emotions. Another tactic is to push unwanted emotions to one-side and use distraction to ignore them, rather than listen and find out the cause of the disturbance. When we are feeling stressed or upset, we may turn on the TV to take our mind off it, or go for a drink with friends. All of these methods of avoidance are employed as a way of crowding out the emotions. It is like having a warning light come on in your car and, instead of dealing with the problem, a piece of tape is placed over it.

In truth we don't want our emotions to stop giving us feedback, rather we want them to inform us of important information, since they are our own warning lights. But we do need to be able to view the advice clearly and act appropriately.

To conclude, the function of the emotions is to aid and inform us when there is something needing our attention. As we learn to listen to them, we begin to find out the true reasons behind their expression. We then gain the ability to understand them more and allow them to be expressed in an integrated and harmonious way.

Letting go of Status, Pride and Selfish Ambition

Much importance is placed on status and vying for position and success in society. I believe these things are mental hindrances. Perhaps if we were to reject all titles, qualifications and physical symbols of rank, class and wealth to focus on the things we truly want to do with our lives, then we would have a refreshing sense of freedom.

The longer I spend contemplating society, the more I am convinced that most of us spend our entire lives in struggle. We desperately try to build a sense of self without realising that is all temporary, that what we are putting our time and effort into will only disappear. So it is far more important to let go of this futile task, this building up of something that can't be maintained, and to instead focus on the more important aspects of life. You cannot make yourself so important, so special you don't die. All that will remain is your effect on the world. The fruits of your labours.

Train Your Mind as You Would Your Body

Wouldn't it be wonderful if we trained our minds like we train our bodies?

If you visit the gym you will see a vast array of different types of training equipment. Treadmills, cardiovascular machines and cycles for training your heart and lungs; weights to lift and train your supporting muscles; and machines where you can focus on pure strength. Nowadays, gyms tend to have lots of innovative functional apparatus that allow you to train your body to be able to apply the training to real life. If you look at us as a race you can see that we all instinctively know that physical training can heal us. So if we injure a part of our body, the very first thing we do is start to move it, to check out where the injury is and to establish the problem area. We then start to look for ways to fix it and we are happy to share such knowledge. So, if we have bad posture or a sore back we recommend to each other particular exercises which will help correct the injury, or one which repeats the correct type of movement. We are happy to adjust our posture in daily life and change the way we move.

If we would do the same with our mind, I think the world would be a very different place. Imagine a world where it was normal to practice changing your state of mind, to train it to work better in your daily life. For example, you could practice dealing with depression by getting a timer and seeing how long you can feel happy about something and keep practicing to improve your skill, working up second by second. Imagine a circumstance where we change our attitude just like we change our posture, where we train our mental strength, flexibility and coordination just the same as we train our physical bodies.

In society there is a bit of a taboo about mental illness, so we are less likely to talk to people about our emotional problems than if we had a sore knee. But what if we approach these two problems in the same way? Perhaps there is an emotion that you feel very uncomfortable with, or find very hard to experience. To strengthen the emotion you would need to practice experiencing it to help bring it into balance. For example, if you found it hard to cry, you could watch sad films or read old Greek tragedies. In this way you would be able to heal it, or become proficient in expressing that emotion. I think this would bring balance to ourselves and thus to our society.

Contemplate this suggestion, look at any areas in your mental functioning that you believe could be improved. Think about how you train them and how you can improve them the same way you would train something to do with the body. This approach I believe can lead to a greater balance which will spread out from ourselves to the rest of the world.

CHAPTER: 11
How to Deal With Negative Thoughts or Images

This chapter addresses the difficulties that can be encountered when dealing with negative mental images and thoughts. This includes worries or concerns that are irrational and devoid of any real purpose, or meaning, and are unrelated to anything we need to deal with. They sometimes manifest as repetitive thoughts or imaginings, and are usually of a frightening or repulsive nature. They may enter into our mind's eye and continue in their repetition. This is not such an uncommon experience as you may think. As we develop our imagination, intuition and compassion, this is a challenge we may well be facing at some point along our path.

Often when we experience these thoughts or images, the natural response is to avoid them. We try to push them away and to find ways to prevent them returning, because we find them so disturbing. Conversely, due to the level of concern and worry, there may be a tendency to dwell on them.

The very fact you are concerned about these thoughts returning often causes a fear that draws them in and leads them to repeat in the mind's eye. This repetition of the worrying thought creates more concern. This pattern of behaviour creates a negative cycle, whereby the more we attempt to escape, the more we are drawn into it. In psychological terms this is known as Coué's Law of Reversed Effort. But how can we break this cycle and turn the situation to our advantage?

From experience and practice, I would advise that you employ three important and powerful principles.

The First Principle:
Do not feel bad about feeling bad

If you are plagued by a certain subject of concern, it is a natural and understandable reaction to feel emotions such as regret and guilt. Sometimes, when we have repeated worries, we can get so caught up in a subject that we start to mistakenly associate ourselves with it. Confused and misunderstanding what is happening, we may even begin to question our own character or sense of morals.

It is also important to note firstly, you are the observer (the one doing the worrying), not that which is being observed (the subject of the worry). Secondly, the reason why you are dwelling on that subject is because you find that image or thought shocking and unpalatable, therefore in-congruent to your own nature. The emotions you are experiencing reflect the correct reaction - you should dislike these kind of things. If something is scary and we become fearful, this is perfectly correct. If something is repulsive and you find yourself responding accordingly, this is also the correct course of action. It is the unnecessary dwelling on such subjects which is unproductive.

The Second Principle:
Understanding the purpose of worry and why it it can be a good thing

When disturbing images or thoughts arise unbidden, it is easy to start to question yourself and wonder such things as, 'If I can't control my own mind, then what kind of person am I?' Or even if there is something wrong with you. So let us consider why a perfectly healthy mind may sometimes think it necessary to do this.

It seems that under some circumstances this is a mechanism the mind uses to check the warning systems. I have experienced this under extreme conditions when my body and mind are undergoing huge hardship. To explain, imagine instead a fire alarm in a building. We want to know that it will go off and warn us in the event of a fire, but in order to ensure it is working well, we must test it by intentionally setting it off. To then ensure that everyone would be safe if there was a fire, we also practice the fire drill when this happens, with everyone in the building practising how to exit calmly and safely before lining up outside. By flashing these images or thoughts, the mind is also testing our reactions, checking that we respond in a suitable manner. This means that if the alarm goes off and it's not a drill, we are prepared.

The Third Principle:
Correct your mind

We are constantly having to correct and update our minds in everyday life. Think of how many times you have viewed something from the distance and thought it to be an animal or person, only to find on closer inspection it is actually nothing of the sort, maybe just a plant of some kind moving in the wind. If it is dark and we are alone, we may even respond with fear initially, but with the new information we adjust and correct our mind accordingly. Similarly, if we have an inappropriate urge or emotion that is out of place we also need to do the same.

At some points in our lives we will need to police our mind more strongly and this maybe one of those times for you. So when a negative thought appears with no apparent cause for alarm, say for example if you were worried that you were going to scald yourself, correct the thought. So with this particular example, whenever that thought came into your mind you could correct it with a phrase such as, 'I am safe and will use this as a reminder to be careful with hot water' or 'I am skillful and aware and able to avoid danger'. This allows us to start to transform the workings of our mind and to utilise our worry for our own betterment. Once you have done this move your thoughts on to other matters. Whenever it floats into your mind correct with the positive suggestion and then let go. Do this each and every time that worry occurs and you will find that it gets easier and easier, until your mind starts to correct the thought before it has even fully formed.

Not only are we building up a positive battery, but by using this method it allows us to take action and turn a negative thought or image into something that can be used in a correct, empowering and positive way. Just like not feeling bad about having negative thoughts, this action takes away the power of the negative thought, because you are not worried about it occurring. In fact, this wonderful technique actually starts to turn around the worry to your advantage. So every time a negative thought comes up, it is an opportunity to dwell on the opposite and practice correcting your mind. In this way the worry can be viewed as a positive reminder.

This principle can also be applied to our words and actions, to instigate positive change to other aspects of our lives. If you say or do anything incorrectly, note the mistake as a learning process, as something not to be repeated and eloquently restate your position with greater clarity. So, if you say something hurtful, correct it. If you drop rubbish on the floor, pick it up. As with our thoughts, the correction is only meaningful if it is applied whenever necessary.

The more you do this, the more you will find that your mind starts to do this automatically. Soon the negative thoughts will barely occur and yet the positive thoughts will continue repeating.

Using the combination of all these exercises will ensure effective strategies are put in place, which will aid in stopping the formation of potential negative cycles. All thoughts have a particular energy and charge, which over time builds up a momentum. Using these practices in daily life will ensure the momentum is moving in the direction you want. Your worry becomes your tool for transformation. It is an opportunity to correct thoughts or imaginings that cause you concern, thus empowering you to tackle and challenge these negative forces each and every time they occur. By doing this you will find that it becomes easier to deal with and eventually becomes habitual.

It's understandable that anyone dealing with worrying thoughts would very much like the problem to just go away in an instant. For those embarking on the process of letting go of worry it is very important to note the following quote from the great zen master Dogen.

'No matter how bad a state of mind you may get into, if you keep strong and hold out, eventually the floating clouds must vanish and the withering wind must cease.'

Once you start to apply these techniques to your life it will take time for your thinking patterns to change. Correcting the mind is a skill and requires practice, but, as your skill grows, you will find yourself improving at an increased speed. Let time pass and don't worry about worrying. Rather, reassure yourself you are doing all you can and that each and every time you redirect your thoughts in the right direction you are making progress. Remember that with every day that passes you are creating positive, automatic thoughts to replace the negative ones. Because of this you have no reason to fear or be concerned about a worry or negative thought entering your mind.

Also, remember that during this time every thought you have about a pleasant or positive subject is a victory, so be sure to fill your life with positive activities and time with people that uplift you. Once you have everything in place, it is important to be patient and to rest. Often these difficulties occur during periods of great trial and tiredness, and it may be that the reasons your mind misidentified the risk in the first place was due to the level of fatigue you were experiencing. With this new outlook it allows you to gain a fresh perspective, to receive the kind of recovery that you need to get back on top of the situation and bring you back into balance. This then allows you to start to function naturally.

Often people who have a period of anxiety and worry in their life feel bad about it. They feel like they have wasted their time or had a period of life stolen from them, please be assured that there are great advantages to the training involved in overcoming this problem. You will find that through the techniques listed in this chapter your consciousness becomes more refined and controlled. In a sense, your training in correcting and directing your mind has been a form of mental discipline, giving you the ability to make other adjustments in your life. For example, refraining from speaking when needed, or adjustments regarding diet and exercise. Many people who have mastered their minds with this method find their abilities far excel that of their fellow man once they have recovered.

And finally please remember that the mark of someone's mental health is their ability to recover from problems, not whether or not the circumstances in life have led to them in to difficulty in the first place.

Harmonising Disruptive Thoughts

In addition to what has already been covered in dealing with negative thoughts, here is an exciting insight I have had as to the ideal method of correcting and redirecting the mind. This technique is both beautiful in its simplicity and magnificent in its ease and effectiveness.

This can be used in circumstances where you have negative automatic thoughts or imaginings that you would rather not have, or when you are trying to change your behaviour, but the habitual thought patterns are getting in the way of your new goals. This is for those times where the thoughts are particularly persistent and immovable. I have found this to work when other techniques won't.

One circumstance where this technique could be particularly useful is when dealing with negative self-speak. So, every time a person attempts a task the phrases they repeat to themselves are focused on why they cannot do it, or maybe why they shouldn't, or, even worse, why they don't deserve to for some reason. When trying to succeed this is very counterproductive and tends to be particularly difficult to counteract.

It could be someone who has a negative vision of the future and who just keeps picturing things going wrong. Or even someone who has imaginings which are horrific, or worrying appearing in their mind's eye, without them wanting them to be there. We can also imagine this technique is useful for someone who wants to do something different in their life, but keeps visualising thoughts that are the opposite to what they are doing. Maybe someone who is trying to lose weight but keeps thinking about the food they would rather be eating.

Often the popular methods recommend combatting the thought by using the opposite. So by changing the tone from an authoritative one to something silly, or a voice warning of 'doom and gloom' to a happy one. Or if the negative thought appears visually, to picture the same scene positively. The technique I am about to describe takes this same idea to its logical conclusion - to seek balance by using the opposite sense to that which is out of control.

I have found that using a different sense to change the negative emotion to be a more effective approach and one that brings about success with far less effort. For example, if you are suffering from negative self-speak, you could fill yourself with a feeling of success, imagining that feeling as it washes over you. Or you could visualise how beautifully things are going to go. Likewise, if you have negative images come into your mind, rather than fight that straight on by trying to override the image with another, you want to take that energy and redirect it into an affirmation. So, if you are fearful that your health is at risk and keep having images of harm coming your way, you could change it to an affirmation, repeating to yourself, "I am completely healthy." This technique is extremely effective, but it is important to let go of the original negative stimuli, or automatic thought, and instead to dwell on the new one. Then just let go and carry on with your life. If you find the counterproductive thought appears, correct it again. Make sure you enjoy the correction far more than you are concerned about the original negative thought.

I have also found this holds true to helping others. If someone is having a hard time with something in their mind, look for what sense they are using and make sure you move them out of that sense. So this could be using visualisation, affirmations, imagining a feeling this kind of thing. But it can also be in a practical way. If someone has a worrying feeling in their body rather than offering to rub their shoulders make them a cup of tea, get them to listen to some calming music or put something uplifting on the television. If someone has seen something horrific and is caught in a repetitive cycle of playing it through their mind, this is a circumstance where talking could work best. Use a calming tone and audio rather than visual terms. In this way I believe you can take the negative force and can transform it without going into battle with it head on. Often people in a state of shock or tiredness can get so caught up in the hardship, or the negative thought pattern, that any interaction with it just leads them deeper into that circumstance. This technique I find to be extremely effective myself and I hope you too will benefit from this.

CHAPTER: 12

A Spiritual Person's Guide to Dealing with Negative People

It is important to be clear what is meant by 'negative people'. This does not refer to people who we may find uncomfortable or difficult to deal with, maybe someone who is incompetent and continually makes mistakes that affects us, or causes us to feel a degree of frustration. Nor does it refer to someone you dislike because you do not share the same interests, or are not naturally in harmony with them. Let me be absolutely clear, I am referring to people whose primary purpose is to empower themselves by dis-empowering and hurting others.

This kind of behaviour has normally come about because they have given up on improving themselves. Since they believe they cannot change to make things better in their own life, they start to hurt others and try to bring them down instead. This normally comes about when a person becomes trapped by a particular emotion or method of dealing with problems. Confused and unable to see why they should change, instead they look to blame those around them. From where they are standing, it is easier to rise by knocking others down, than to improve the self and rise through their own character.

When somebody like this comes into contact with you in your life, what do you do?

Firstly, if possible, it is advisable to avoid dealing with them completely. There may be a natural urge to try to help people who are in a situation that is ineffective for them, but in my experience the perception trap is so strong, anything you do will normally backfire. To understand why this is the case, we need to consider reality from their point of view.

Often these kinds of people are trapped in a world of battle. They view life through the lens of conflict and understand all interaction as either those fighting for or against them - there is no place for neutral. In society you will see this on a very basic level as neighbours compete over belongings, friends compete with each other over popularity, work colleagues compete over who has the greater status at work, etc. If a person perceives the world in this way, an assumption is made that everyone else must also have the same viewpoint. Thus any action is seen in terms of competition and conflict. It is difficult for them to perceive anyone as having a genuinely positive motive. For example, if someone tells them about something good that has happened in their life, the person trapped by conflict will only be able to view it in a negative way and will most likely see it as an attempt to prove superiority. Or if offered assistance, they will view it suspiciously, assuming it is a way to show them up by demonstrating their need for help. Each and every action is seen as an aggressive act in need of retaliation.

If you do gain the trust of someone who is in this emotional world, it is useless to try to convince them the world is otherwise. No matter what you say, or how clearly you try to explain to them this is not the case, they will not believe you. This is because they themselves act this way and so they simply believe that others have the same motives as them, but lie about it. So, when they try to help someone it is to prove they are better in some way. Because of this they find it hard to understand others and judge the actions of people by their own perception. For this reason I would strongly recommend you do not try to assist them. Because of their tainted viewpoint they will misunderstand your intentions and believe that you are willing to be an ally to help them battle against other people. And as soon as they realise this is not the case (which may take a very long time because of their own programming), they will feel you have turned on them and deserted them. To people such as these, if you are not on their side, you must be against them.

Another very common trapping, is to be caught up in a sense of lack. People in this state feel they never have enough; whether it's enough friends, enough money, enough respect, enough security or enough status. And they are so desperate and scared, that as soon as they do get some, they use it up for fear of it going, and in doing so, cause the lack they so fear.

If you become close to a person trapped by lack you will notice that they often complain that others do not make enough of an effort, or that eventually everyone abandons them. It is difficult to not be drawn into their world because it may seem that they are in need of help and have been let down by those around them. Their craving for attention may at first appear to be harmless, or even flattering, but this situation is unsustainable as their constant demands sap up your energy. Sometimes they may want assistance from you with a particular problem or area of their life, but once this is solved the demands will not stop.

Eventually one of three things will happen; either you will believe you have helped them as best you can and handover responsibility back to them; or you will run out of resources; or simply not meet their expectations. In the first case they will not view this positively since it means you are withdrawing attention, which is what they are really after. Whereas you believed that the goal was to assist them in gaining self-sufficiency, they never really wanted independence and will feel hurt and rejected. This may manifest in ways that at first seem strange, such as barriers or behaviour to sabotage your efforts. In the second and third cases they will see this as as proof that you simply do not care enough. When this happens they will see you as yet another person who has failed them.

As you can see, the person is caught in an emotional trap and in reality does not want to change. In these situations it is advisable not to interact with them at all.

In life, you will inevitably face unavoidable situations where you may encounter these kinds of people. If you have to interact with the type of person who attacks others and dis-empowers them (be it very subtly in their approach), here is some advice on how best to address this circumstance.

First protect yourself. Be careful not to be pulled into their world and try to keep them at a distance, emotionally if it's not possible physically. To do this you may have to limit what personal information you tell them, and even, in extreme circumstances, feed them with misinformation.

Observe them to see what they covet. It is possible to understand someone by what they want. However, be careful to pay attention to their actions rather than their words, since this will show the truth. Once you understand them you will be in a better position to predict their actions and understand their motives, helping you to protect yourself from their actions and keep control of the situation.

Often these people have an inner conflict that can manifest itself in a number of ways, usually through emotional drama. Their need for emotional highs means they will create extreme situations. Any emotion can become the focal viewpoint, since for them a negative reaction is better than none. The difficulty in this situation is creating an environment where you are not pulled about by their dramas. You will find that if you refuse to play their games, they will soon turn their attention elsewhere. Be warned that it may get worse before it gets better, especially as this may be a game they've played all their life and you are still learning. You may also be the first person who has stood up to them, and it may take a while for them to realise it's not working.

If you do want to help, please be aware that unless you can move them to a completely new environment, all you can do is offer gentle suggestions, a nudge in the right direction, or a hint of another possibility.

When you next interact with them make sure any suggestions you make are the next step for them. This is really important. From outside it is often easy to see what solution will cure the problem completely, but for someone who is caught in that trap, medicine will look like poison. So we need to look at how they interact with the world and very subtly guide them in a direction that is empowering for them, but at the same time gently buys into their world view. This is important because they will not hear your message unless it is in their language.

Remember to tread with caution and do not let them cease full control, otherwise you will end up in the same realm, or the same emotional trap they are in. So be clear in what you want from this person, restrict the amount of contact you have, and make sure you do not become a part of their world, the area they completely control. If possible try to move your interactions into an environment outside of their sphere of influence.

Under the guidance of an experienced teacher, it is possible for someone caught in a negative mindset to turn the tables and use the force of the aggression, desire or doubt as the key to their own freedom. However, this takes a lot of co-operation and a skilful guide.

Finally, try to benefit from having to interact with this kind of person. At first this may seem preposterous, but you can learn to use contact with negative people as a form of training.

In Tibetan monasteries it is a known technique to assign a training partner to monks undergoing meditation training. The role is quite different to how you may at first imagine it to be, and often involves banging on the wall or causing other distractions to frustrate the monk. This is meant to help him learn to overcome the emotions of frustration and distraction. In Japan, a similar form of training is employed in some monasteries, where the monks are forced to eat their food at high speed.

So too can you view this person you must deal with as your training partner, someone who will challenge you and test your ability to put what you have learnt into practice. Your goal in this test is to bring about a harmonious outcome for everyone involved. If you think about it, you will not find any training partner more diligent than this one. By applying this approach to your day, you can benefit from these circumstances in your life.

How to Deal with Negative Wishes or Influences from Others

In life you may come across people who have, for whatever reason, ill intentions towards you. They may not be doing anything in particular, but you feel that their thoughts and feelings to you are affecting you adversely. It is unwise to engage with this person in a battle on their own terms, but there are strategies you can use to deal with them.

The most common form for this type of attack to take is an intention to see you suffer. Because of this it is possible to give them what they want whilst benefiting you. Let me explain, they are so blinded by their hate that they will interpret any negative emotion received from you as success on their part, without questioning what it could really mean.

So if they are wanting to feel your pain, let go of your pain and let them have it. Or weakness, or fear, or hurt, or whatever else they are after. In this way, you will rid yourself of the aspects holding you back and they will believe they have won.

You will find that this is quite an interesting solution, because the person attacking you actually wants the things you are sending to them, albeit in a confused sort of way. They even do all the work to create that connection with you, and so when they receive these feelings, it is a positive outcome to them and they initially see this as success in their goals. You, of course can fully release these negative emotions and be healed as they redouble their efforts.

Whatever form the attack comes in, a useful way to view it is to think of it as if it were the dustbin man arriving, or imagine it like the bacteria being put on the compost heap. Then move your mind to the list of things you wish to let go of and let them go! Once this process has been completed, forcibly move your attention to other matters.

This allows you to focus all your energy on the positive things in your life, which is really important. You become like the sun, you are completely regular in your life, you cannot be stolen from or hurt, the light simply shines out. No one can steal the sunlight, it is given away. This is the most powerful way to deal with this circumstance. The more you contemplate this, the more you realise without knowing it, these people who are involved in these negative activities are actually involved in a blessing. If you use these strategies that are listed, you will help them find the true purpose for their actions.

Crown of Thorns

Once when visiting a church in Budapest, I witnessed a ceremony involving a procession of men dressed in the uniforms of the Knights Templar and carrying a set of relics. These were said to be the crown of thorns, a shard of the true cross and a nail that had been through the hand of Jesus.

Despite having heard the Christian story of the cross many times, the universal symbolism suddenly became clear to me. These were statements not just about the life of Jesus, but about the path we all walk when we try to be the good in the world, the light in the dark. The cross is the weight we must bear, the nails the pain we must endure, but what moved me most was the crown of thorns. It made me think about the story of Jesus on a different level.

It made me think of Rosicrucianism and the famous lines from Mozart's magic flute, 'our path is like the rose because it has thorns'. Anyone reading this who is on the path of spiritual development and the cultivation of virtue will instantly recognise the symbolism of the crown of thorns that we are all forced to wear, as we continue to face ourselves and move towards our higher goals. The closer you get to your goals the more the outside world seems to mock and belittle you.

As the crown of thorns processed before the image of Mary, Mother of God, I found myself thinking of her, as a symbol for this ability we have inside us to be reborn and to change who we are inside; to die and to become something better than before. Were the nails, the shard of the cross and the crown of thorns genuine? I don't know if they were, but is this important when they have the power to inspire even one man to embrace the hardship and push on to the greater good?

CHAPTER: 13

How to Turn Procrastination & Inner Conflict to Your Advantage

It is early morning and the alarm sounds, reminding you it is time to get up to do your practice - be it yoga, meditation, or to go for a run. This is a goal you have thought about and have decided that you really want to do. When you went to bed you were determined you would get up and spring into action, yet the warmth of the bed calls and you find it difficult to motivate yourself to get up. You may find all manner of inner objections rise up to try and prevent you from fulfilling your chosen goal. Perhaps a more agreeable and easier suggestion will come to mind as a way to put off the goal until later. It is that moment of inner conflict which I call the sticking point.

It is this aspect we will be looking at and how we can turn internal objections, or sticking points, around to be used for our own empowerment. That moment, instead of being a roadblock in your attempt to fulfil your goal, it can actually be flipped and become a moment you can push off from, using the energy to create momentum to achieve your goal.

These techniques can be used for any form of discipline. Not only can they be used with an ongoing action such as meditation practice, exercise or study, but this approach can also be used for mundane or tedious tasks such as accounts.

So let us imagine that you decide to tackle an activity on Sunday afternoon. However, when Sunday afternoon arrives suddenly you find that there are all sorts of reasons why you should put it off, maybe until later or even next week. You are reminded that you have friends that want to see you, or maybe you have something far more compelling that draws you away from your intended activity. Soon you find yourself being pulled away from the task, so what can you do to stay on target?

The first stage in overcoming the objections that prevent you from carrying out your will is to identify each one and which ones tend to win. Then you can tackle the objection using the method best suited. You will find that they come in three broad categories.

1. A Confused Approximation of the Goal

This is where an alternative is offered to the original goal with the suggestion that it is not really an alternative, but that it does in fact fulfil the original aim. An example of this could be a person deciding to do their morning meditation routine lying down, rather than sitting up as they usually would. There could be all sorts of justifications, but the truth is this person is looking to avoid getting out of bed.

If this happens to you, next time pay careful attention and you will find there is a small moment of rational thought that informs you of the true intention. So in the above example there is likely to be a flash of insight that in fact by taking that course of action the person will most likely fall asleep, not meditate. But then the inner conflict comes up with a rational argument as to why this would be an acceptable approach and proceeds to convince the mind that meditating in bed is a good idea. For someone wanting to exercise each morning, they may find themselves reasoning, 'Well, I walked around town all day yesterday so, I do not feel it is necessary to go for a run this morning because I already exercised lots. I will sleep in.'

This kind of reasoning is a confused approximation since the mind tries to convince us that the replacement activity is equivalent to the original. This works especially well when we have mixed intentions about the original goal. From outside it is plain to see that these suggestions are irrational and seem somewhat ridiculous to us, however the mind can be extremely creative when it comes to procrastination.

Overcoming this barrier has a lot to do with not giving it time to get a hold. But first identify whether there is a genuine reason. If, for example, you are finding it difficult to do your morning routine because you always find yourself tired in the morning, consider whether you should in fact be going to bed earlier. Next make sure the goal is very clearly defined in your mind and what would constitute success, be cautious to ensure it is achievable. Once you have done this you will find it easier to move your focus back on track. So you can use the approximation as a reminder to focus on the purpose and value in your goal, and in this way you will find it aids your motivation.

2. Negative Self-Speak

This one is pretty much self-explanatory. Rather than encouraging yourself, your self-speak demotivates and belittles you and your efforts.

Here are a list of some examples:
- I can't do this
- I will only fail

- It won't make any difference, so why am I bothering?

- I am stupid for even thinking this was a good idea in the first place.

- I was never the clever one at school, so I won't pass the exam

- I will only make myself look like a fool

You know you are in this category, when the main reason for not attempting to go through with the activity is an overwhelming negative feeling and, in extreme cases, self loathing. This isn't just shown just in the words said, but also in the tone used and images that may manifest.

One way to test this is to imagine if you would use the same phrasing and tone to someone else in a similar circumstance. If this was your best friend attempting to improve their life, then would you say the same things? This exercise sometimes exposes just how tough we are being on ourselves.

The best way to tackle negative self speak is to first change the tone used. This can be done in two ways. Sometimes simply changing the tone will make the statement supportive. 'Come on', for example, can be said in a disparaging and sarcastic manner to discourage you from the action, yet by changing the tone it becomes encouraging and supportive. However, if the wording itself cannot be changed, then adjust the tone to take power away from the voice. Mickey Mouse is a particularly good choice for this, since it is hard to take anything he may say particularly seriously!

Use this as a way to practice self speak and correct your inner voice to the ideal tone. In this way you will gain an inner supporter and ally.

3. Dismissal of the Goal

The rationalisation by the mind of why a particular goal should not be completed can be quite creative, and sometimes it can take some careful analysing and unravelling to see the truth. Below are some excuses you may have encountered, we will look at each one to determine what the reality of the situation is and how to bring yourself back on target.

One common excuse is finding a reason for why today is an exception and the goal is in some way harmful or counterproductive. For example, 'I was ill last night so I won't run today. Better to rest when you are ill, so I recover quickly and then can run once I'm better.' In this case the reason given is that by running the person will make themselves feel worse and the implication is that by not running today, they will be able to run sooner. However, often the reality is that our own assessment of the situation is coloured by our inner conflict. So in the warm bed we decide we are too ill to get up and go outside where it is cold, deciding instead to stay tucked up. Actually, if we got up and ready to go, then we would be in a better position to decide whether the concern is legitimate.

Rather than using the objection as a reason to stop training, it can be used to enhance our discipline. Training is most valuable under adversity, since life rarely stops and when we train we are practising for real life. So, if you are ill and concerned that a run would be too tough, then go for a restorative walk. If you feel tired and are concerned you will not be able to meditate, then use that tiredness as your training. Learning to focus through tiredness is an important skill practised in different spiritual traditions throughout the world.

One reason students often give for avoiding a particular exercise is that they have in someway already completed it; they are now on to higher and more difficult things. Counterintuitively, you will find the more challenging the undertaking the more likely some people will decide that is too easy as a means to not do it. By deciding, 'I have already learnt this, it is beneath me,' they are avoiding a risk of failure without admitting weakness.

The easiest way to counter this is to turn the argument on its head, to say, 'If this is so easy, then it will be no bother for me to do it.' If you find yourself still resistant, then you may have found the area you need to work on the hardest.

To Review

1. Are you coming up with some change of plan that involves change to what you said you were going to do?

2. Are you talking to yourself negatively?

3. Are you coming up with rationalisations for not doing it at all?

Once these patterns of behaviour have been identified it becomes easier to know which areas need a degree of focus. This becomes a wonderful form of training whereby you use these very objections as your motivation. Think of a martial artist who uses the strength of an opponent to twist around and throw him.

As you practice you will find the negative-speak, or the approximation, or the rationalisation of dismissal actually starts lessening.

If you find yourself procrastinating about achieving that goal and putting it off till tomorrow then the time to act is NOW. Say to yourself, 'I am going to do this NOW.'

When faced with a creative 'solution', be sure to turn the logic around on itself. So if you decide, 'I am going to do my meditation in bed because it's harder,' instead question the logic. Clearly it's not harder, otherwise you would up already and practising. If it feels harder to get up then use the initial reason for staying in bed to motivate you to get up. Let us challenge ourselves then and do what is really more difficult.

Or, if the task seems too easy then perhaps think to yourself, 'If I am a great master then this should be a triviality. Let's just do it.'

The key is, to make the objection part of the solution. With practice you will find your own way of converting whatever your negative or internal objections are into positive outcomes.

This allows us to override our negative programming.

Awareness of Consequences

Another powerful method that can be employed is to associate the negativity with the consequences of failing to do the action. However, it is important to keep this as a healthy motivator to ensure the goal is achieved, as it can easily move into harmful areas.

Of course in an ideal world we would only ever use positive motivators. So if we were trying to eat more healthily then we may remind ourselves that healthy eating means that we have more energy to do the things we love. However, the mind often leans towards more of a negative focus. If this is carefully controlled then it can be used. For example, if we are trying to eat more healthily because the doctor has warned us that we are at risk of a heart attack, then we use that as a reminder when we are thinking of deviating from the goal.

But, as I said before, it is important to be careful with this approach. For some people this can very easily become negative self-speak. This is especially true for those who already have tendencies towards negative self-speak and so shouldn't be used by them. An example where this has gone wrong would be if we started to attack our image or personality, trying to shame ourselves into eating healthier. This can be successful in the short term, but over time becomes a very unproductive approach. If you find yourself doing this, then I recommend you avoid this course of action altogether. It is actually not a good long term method, because you are programming the negative self-speak into your consciousness.

Remember, always associate the negative outcome to the negativity that is getting in the way. This is a very important principle to note because then the association remains correct and your positive action is clear and free from negative emotional attachment.

CHAPTER: 14
Learning from an Inner Resistance to Learning

I would like to share some interesting observations, which I hope once contemplated will lead to some meaningful insights. These are behaviours I have seen in myself and others, which I think are fascinating and reveal more about the inner workings of the mind and about goal confusion, among many other things.

Picture this, a martial arts class where people have travelled from all over the world to attend. They have invested a lot of time, money and effort to train with an instructor who they know can teach them what they wish to learn. They know he has great experience with guiding people and he has superior knowledge on how to achieve the goals they are seeking from him, yet I have observed a strange phenomenon.

People were told to practice a technique in a certain way for so many repetitions. Yet, when the instructor stopped looking, they stopped practicing. Between pairs engaging in this strange behaviour I could see there was a sense of achievement, as if there was a one upmanship over the instructor by not doing what he had asked them to do. To me this was absolutely fascinating, as the truth of the situation was that they were paying for a lesson they were deliberately avoiding. Surely they could have sent the money and stayed at home? Thus avoiding the lesson entirely, since that seemed to be their wish. It left me with some questions:

Why would someone make such an effort to go to a class if not to embrace the actual tuition?

And why does it feel like an achievement if they cheat the system and get less from the class?

So it was that I contemplated what I had observed and realised that, to a greater or lesser degree, this resistance to learning happens in many different ways.

I have seen people who want to learn from a particular spiritual tradition and have gone to great efforts to find the right path and teacher. Again, spending a great amount of time and effort searching out for a person they are confident knows how to guide them to achieve their path. They have gone through various trials set by their teacher to prove they are serious, paid to be a student and studied the source material. Yet, when it comes to the syllabus and the teacher asks them to follow a training regime, the student gets upset and complains, saying, 'Why are you trying to control me?' So they have gone to all this effort to gain an expert guide through the mountains and then they do not want to be told which route to walk.

Sometimes you see this manifest in a slightly different way. Someone goes to a teacher, but the student puts up a barrier to learning by trying to control the situation. This is normally to do with their self esteem, especially if they are new to a group and trying to establish dominance. I have seen a whole class disrupted by a student showing different martial arts they used to do. Rather than learn, their agenda is to show how much they know.

This resistance can also appear when the real goal has nothing to do with learning. So the person attending a class may really be wanting a community or friends. It is easy to spot a person like this in the group, since they want to be a part of it but will seem disinterested in learning. They like to be there and around the people, but they pay little attention to any teaching, or the purpose of the group. Instead they are easily distracted and their engagement with the group centres around social interaction. For most people this aspect is present, but the importance differs.

Once we have contemplated this on the lower levels, we can look at this same resistance to learning on the larger scale. Here nature is the teacher, and life is the syllabus. As we grow, both on the mundane and awareness levels, we learn more about how the world works. However, we can see the same patterns if we observe ourselves and others around us. An attempt to control the world rather than be controlled, when we know the rules are not subjective. Or instead of engaging with the difficulties of life and learning to overcome them, attempting to avoid and prove competence in other areas. Or misidentifying the goal, so instead of learning to survive together, we attempt to dominate.

CHAPTER: 15
The Seed of Something Beautiful

I have come to believe that some of our worst qualities and greatest vices, are in fact the seeds of our most important virtues, our greatest potential and all we need to do is to learn how to cultivate those seeds and help them mature into what they are meant to be.

If you ask someone to do something which is difficult for them, or very new, they will often find an approximation of their intended goal. This may occur with someone who starts to learn yoga, but is new to exercise and therefore lacking in flexibility. If they attempt to perform a posture which requires them to put their arms over their head, they may find that they do not have the range of movement to comfortably bring their arms straight above their head and so the hands will be out of alignment. To compensate they may well angle the hands up and will be convinced that they are performing the correct posture. Often they are not aware of this and feel the goal has been achieved. So they may inadvertently hurt themselves whilst thinking they are in fact improving their health. It would be wrong to stop them from practising because of this, instead it would be better to encourage them to continue improving their practice until it becomes what they were aiming for all along.

This is also evident in life, we tend to work according to our nature and we often choose careers that reflect that. However, if we are given a task that is outside our remit of experience, we often use our previous experience and a way we already know works. So in order to use a method that we know works for us to achieve the intended goal, we change it to suit our nature. For example, if we are asked to do a job that involves a lot of stamina and meticulous attention, but our natural strengths are of a more energetic and strong nature, we may perform the task with haste. Although we complete it, we are likely to miss the important details required for the completion of the task to the same standard that a slower and more detailed person would reach.

Often our negative expressions are due to the fact we have yet to develop the required skills in that area. To compensate, we apply the same old strategies for dealing with new situations, but find that they do not work and this may produce a negative reaction or feeling.

As we grow and develop we realise that certain situations require certain responses which are appropriate for that moment. To illustrate, being assertive in a business environment is necessary to achieve results, but not helpful when dealing with a mourning relative, which requires a degree of tact and gentleness. If we have not developed the ability to adapt to different environments, we may find it difficult to switch between different modes of behaviour. This lack of flexibility can often be perceived as a negative quality, but in truth the individual has yet to learn the necessary skill. Perhaps in this situation they have not yet realised that assertiveness is not always the best way to bring someone's focus away from a negative emotion outside of the working environment, and the importance of being gentle and kind.

Inflammation in the body is analogous to this. The body experiences inflammation when it perceives a foreign entity, or when the body becomes injured it acts as a way to protect itself from further harm. However, if this intention becomes misplaced an autoimmune response will activate whereby the body starts to attack itself thinking its own cells are the foreign entity. So the body is doing its best to protect itself, but in fact it has made an error. The personality operates in a similar fashion. It may act in a way that it thinks is beneficial, but in fact, acts more of a hindrance to the outcome it is trying to create. An example of this would be someone, who genuinely wants people to respect them. They want to set an example and to be of benefit to the world, to be the person others see doing the right thing. This expression may manifest in the desire to become famous at all costs.

In another circumstance, maybe someone wishes to create a beautiful environment for people and wants to make the world better place. They also wish to protect the people they love around them. This desire for beauty may direct them onto a path focused on obtaining wealth to fulfill their goal. However, they have forgotten that happiness is the true desire behind their original intention, but become focused on creating a grandiose environment. We all know examples of business people who have made huge amounts of money, yet if you ask why they are still chasing bigger profits and bonuses, they say it is for the home and family. In reality the family have been taken care of, but what is lacking is love, time and presence.

Sometimes, what is a normal positive emotion can turn into a perceived negative one due to an inner confusion. Perhaps the desire to avoid an expression or emotion is a way of dealing with an aspect of life which they find difficult. This is often due to a past negative experience which has imprinted itself onto the mind, and now any experience related to that emotion becomes blanketed with the same negativity. An example of this may be someone who has a perceived negative view of having sexual relations with another person and chooses to renounce this aspect of their life. They decide to be celibate rather than engaging in healthy relationships, maybe to avoid the emotional pain or discomfort that they feel surrounding that area in their life.

In some cases a person may have been hurt emotionally by others in the past saying negative things. A decision is made to join a silent monastic order, to avoid dealing with negative interactions. In this case, it is better for that person to learn how to deal with the negativity from others and learn to conquer these aspects of their personality. The lesson is about empowerment and developing new skills in dealing with life. The personality will often try to find an easy option, an approximation of the goal, because it is a challenge and requires effort to transcend that undeveloped aspect of the personality.

In conclusion, it is understood that the goal is to master these aspects of our personality. To find the genuine cause that lies behind our expression. It is that seed, or beautiful spark, which is our true intention. So often our experiences and emotions colour, misdirect or confuse the manifestation of this intention, but hidden is a seed of our true potential. By finding the true purpose for our actions, we skilfully learn to understand our emotions and learn how to truly give them the highest expression they deserve.

Remember, all emotions have a purpose and find ways to express themselves because they are trying to communicate something significant to us about the situation we are in. This is true even of emotions we tend to label as negative. Just like the warning light in a car, we do not want to hide the warning, but solve the problem. So it is with an emotion, we need to listen to that signal and solve it, so it can be expressed correctly. Often this means pausing rather than following your first instinct, which may be inappropriate and lead away from a good outcome.

In this way we look at what the real purpose behind the emotion is and to utilise that. With this approach we gain the greatest benefit and indeed, this may be the only approach that leads to complete integration in the end.

CHAPTER: 16

Being Open to the Changes You Are Trying to Make

When we work consciously in order to evolve our lives or selves, we need to be open to change. This is true whether we are looking to build success, healing, inner tranquility or contentment. It is important to remember, if you have chosen this as your goal and it is something that is generally lacking in your life, then your habits, views of the world, and internal mechanisms will not be setup to achieve it. These need to change.

Think of these new habits as forming the vessel that can hold the new way and maintain it. Without these changes, the support is not in place and so we either do not realise this transformation, or it slips through our fingers almost as soon as we grasp it. There are various reasons for this. It is not rare for someone who is creating success through energy work and visualisation to continually turn down paid work or business opportunities, which will lead to great wealth for very little effort, as they are looking for their 'magical' solution. People who are working on calmness will sometimes find themselves rejecting situations which will lead to inner tranquility as, without the internal change, they cannot recognise the solution or find it too uncomfortable. It is said that to those who are ill, medicine often looks like poison at first appearances. In some cases, a person who is ill may reject the medicine offered three or four times before accepting it.

Let us imagine that someone who has terrible arthritic problems is offered a place on a course of hydrotherapy. Due to the nature of the illness it is quite hard for them to be motivated. In this situation to get out of bed, to catch the bus, to journey to the swimming pool requires great effort. They might even find themselves fearful of going through the pain that is involved in rehabilitation.

In order to grasp these opportunities, we first need to accept there is a need for change; a change of internal habits and lifestyle. Often we find the most unexpected of changes leads to the solution. Sometimes it's in the small changes to our attitude or perception that offers us the greatest benefits, not in the big ones. Often these opportunities are a chance to alter our perception, more than a chance to solve the problem in one go. If you are doing everything to create that change, be ready to grasp it when it comes along in real life.

CHAPTER: 17

Recovery is the Start of Discipline

The key to discipline does not lie in learning how to try harder. Or forcing yourself into doing more. Quite the contrary, the very first step begins with recovery. If you are disciplined with your recovery, then everything else falls into place. When people find themselves lacking in inspiration and energy they look for all sorts of solutions. This often includes doing more, when in fact it is probably their lack of rest and recovery that is most at fault.

Recovery consists of many different aspects. The first and most foundational aspect is of course sleep. My advice is when you decide to go to sleep, you really do try to sleep. Let me explain. In the modern world technology seeps into all different areas of our lives, including our bedrooms. The bedroom should be kept as a sacred area of rest and recovery, and to allow the intrusion of TVs, computers and even smart phones is detrimental to this. View your nighttime sleep as a time of recovery and really make sure that you prepare properly. Lie down and relax the whole of your body. You can do this by starting at your feet and slowly working up your body, allowing each part to naturally relax as your mind comes to it and let this relaxation bring around healing, which naturally comes with sleep. Focus on your mind coming into balance and harmony automatically during your rest. Some people find warm baths, or other measures helpful. You can experiment with different methods to find the best way for you.

The second area of focus for recovery is your nutrition. I'm sure you already know this, but one of the most important things is to drink enough. Dehydration is one of the biggest barriers to the correct functioning of your body and one of the easiest improvements to make. You will find that even a small increase in your liquid intake will lead to improved energy levels. If you are particularly observant, you may have noticed that the emotions can also become imbalanced when you are dehydrated. So it is important to be fastidious and routined in this. One change I made to my own routine some five years ago, was to drink a pint of water upon waking. I have found the difference incredible and if you only follow one piece of advice, I would suggest you do this.

Regarding eating habits, part of the change in this area involves a shift in your view of each meal. If you start to see food as medicine and only take the food which will cure you of your tiredness and to feed your body correctly, you will find yourself automatically making the right choices. If you master this point of view, you will find yourself increasingly eating a more balanced diet naturally and without having to overcome internal resistance. Really take time to enjoy the food and listen to what your body tells you.

Exercise aids recovery in many different ways. Physically it promotes healing, conditions the body and invigorates the mind. Mentally exercise helps relieve stress and is therapeutic. To achieve these benefits, we need to ensure there is a balance. The exercise needs to be enough to stimulate an adaptation and improvement in the body, but not so much that our bodies cannot keep up. To reiterate, what your body tells you is important, so listen. Exercise to the point you feel a healthy sense of energy, but it is not good to push yourself so far as to cause pain.

Make sure you get lots of mental stimulation as well. Take the time to do things that inspire you, challenge you, and lead to a sense of happiness and harmony. This will help your mind to recover and keep you in the moment.

And finally, it is important to just spend time being. By relaxing and letting the mind clear there is a natural cleansing mechanism that kicks in. Just let time pass and your mind drift. It is important to do this in addition to any form of meditation exercises you do. Allow some free time for the mind to go through its paces and do what it likes.

Once you have developed a firm foundation, then you will find that your discipline in all other areas improves.

CHAPTER: 18

What to do When You do Not Know What You Want in Life

We all go through times in life that can cause us to reassess our priorities. Sometimes this can even lead to our emotions seeming to almost go offline. This occurs most often during a particularly stressful crisis or hardship. Whenever someone talks to me who is going through an experience like this, I tell them of a piece of advice that is given to pilots which works well for life too.

Pilots are warned that there may be times when flying their aeroplane where suddenly something obscures their vision, perhaps some dense cloud (an event that suddenly makes it harder for us to see our path clearly), or they become unsure of their real position, maybe the instrumentation device has malfunctioned (the emotions don't read correctly). Under these circumstances the pilot is advised that it is important to change nothing.

There have been some horrible accidents where inexperienced pilots have noticed their altitude gauges have stopped working whilst in thick cloud. Uncertain of what to do, they have decided it is better to climb, scared that if they don't they will descend dangerously low without realising. So they take the course of action to ascend vertically, but without the instruments to help they misjudge and climb too high, stalling the plane. They assume this is another sensor error, and fail to respond appropriately. So just like when you are driving your car and there is a moment that you cannot see, the best course of action is to continue the route you previously had planned, do not do anything rash.

The same is true of life. If you find you have reached a phase in life where suddenly you find yourself confused and conflicted, where the goals you set previously don't seem useful anymore, then change nothing. In a crisis circumstance keep everything just the same. Think back to when you last had a clear understanding of your purpose here and keep gently working towards that until the clouds clear, or the senses come back.

CHAPTER: 19

Forming a Regular & Balanced Life

One of the most important goals when we choose to follow a spiritual path, or a form of meditation practice for self-improvement, is to develop and establish a balanced life. As we start to exert an effort to establish a routine, life will challenge our qualities, our character and priorities at each step. If you do not develop a balanced lifestyle from the onset, you will find it is a bit like trying to build a castle on sand. We have to keep readjusting the foundations as we continue.

A Balanced Lifestyle Consists of Having:

1. Clear priorities

2. A good social network of positive people around you

3. Harmonious interaction with the world

4. Emotional balance

5. Material affairs completely in order

When trying to harmonise your life, you may find that there are aspects of your personality that challenge you during this process. If this happens understand that this part of your spiritual progress or growth. These are the very aspects of your personality which are the ones you need to balance and harmonise in order to develop.

Some important things to look for are redirection of goals. For instance, you might find in fact, instead of practicing meditation you release that intent by talking about it, watching videos and using the energy to do anything but the actual practice. Sometimes I meet people who research and read copious amounts of literature, but their life is void of practice. This is another form of displacement activity.

Be clear at the start with your intentions when following a spiritual routine. Firstly, know that your spiritual practice is your primary goal in life. And secondly, the dedication to that of practice is at the top of the hierarchy of your priorities. This is the correct order of things, because having a consistent practice allows us to achieve balance in all other levels in life. By making it a priority, it operates like a blessing to the rest of our life in every way.

The next area of life that we wish to address is our social life. This refers to creating harmony with others as far as possible. We want to attract and cultivate friendships that are of a positive nature and support our goals. As we saw earlier, if we must interact with people contrary to our goals then we can see them as training aids, not only learning from their errors but also viewing them as training partners. In this way their attacks or disturbances can be instead viewed as a training exercise for us to practice our new, balanced way of doing things with. If there are any ongoing dramatic areas of your life where things are not solved, it is time to solve them now and try to find a way to have a harmonious existence.

Recovery is a very important thing and to do this well time management is the key. Make sure you develop regular sleeping habits and have enough spare time to recover. The ability to rest and recover, is something that will really pay back investment later on this path. If you find yourself thinking you don't have enough time to recover, then examine how you choose to spend your time. Do you sit in front of the TV flicking through channels for hours? If so make recovery the priority. Or maybe you feel too overworked to get enough rest? If this is the case then you would be surprised by how much your stamina, concentration and ability will improve by sorting out your recovery. There are direct correlations between your mental abilities and whether you are sleeping correctly and regularly. So, it may seem like you are sacrificing work time, but in the long-term it will easily pay off.

There are of course other areas of our lives which are important for us to keep in balance. Often we neglect our emotional needs, so ensure you receive stimulation such as going to beautiful places and doing things you enjoy. If you do find yourself in a particular rut, then try to going for a walk or into the garden everyday, since connecting to the natural world has been proven to help alleviate stress. Make sure that you eat the right things, and exercise regularly to not only keep your body working well, but also to help keep your mental state balanced.

As far as material aspects are concerned, it is important that you set your life up so that you can pay for things in the material world, all matters are in order, and your outside interaction with the world reflects what you want to achieve inside. So make your surroundings beautiful, harmonious and in order. This is important to help ensure these aspects do not unduly interfere with the more important parts of your life.

In order to truly progress, whether with our meditation or in our daily life, it is important to create a balanced platform from which we can begin to work from. This includes developing a regulated and structured life. The best way to do this is to establish a routine that incorporates all your desired goals. Depending on your particular personality you may find that you end up with lots of goals, or perhaps not many at all. If you fall into the former category, try to focus on what is really important to you in life, since having too many goals at once can be counterproductive. If you are unable to cut back on your goals, choose ones to focus on at this moment in your life and write the others down to be completed at a later stage. If you are the type of person who has a vague idea of the direction you are going in, but no set goal this can bring clarity. Producing a clear schedule of your allotted tasks prevents you from feeling overwhelmed, allows you to prioritise, and ensures that you have an honest, congruent, clear vision of what you are trying to do. Sometimes just putting what you want into words is enough to banish inner conflict and counterproductive behaviour.

A method I have found useful is to make appointments with myself for the activities that are important to me, such as meditation or an activity related to one of my goals. Scheduling these as daily tasks means they are not forgotten during the day and also helps me to steadily work towards the goal. Interestingly, when we are dealing with our personality, often we will find one area tends to be more prominent. Mistakenly, this area then becomes the sole focus of the goal and takes precedence over all things in our life. For example, we may decide that our main wish is to become incredibly famous, popular, rich, or fit. These are all noble goals, but they can easily become dominant. We wish to achieve our goals through balance and not by becoming obsessed in a particular area in our life. By using the appointments system it can help to ensure we are dividing our time and effort in a balanced way.

Another consideration we should make is our interaction with others. If we find this area in our life is lacking in harmony, we may need to seek out the imbalance which is causing it. If you find yourself seeking a very strong emotional stimulus, it is usually a sign that you are not recovering fully. Tiredness often dulls the emotions, causing us to seek out stronger responses. Moreover, if we find we are struggling with lack of energy then often we will make poor decisions regarding our choice of words, which can lead to misunderstandings and we tend to be quick to anger or impatience. Likewise, worries about money or material affairs can put unnecessary strain on our relationships, not just romantic ones but also with friends and family. So it is important to get those in harmony in order to be able to see more clearly.

At times of tiredness and high stress, we need to move our focus from high goals and big achievements, to creating a wholesome sense of contentment and harmony in our everyday lives. Then later on we can start thinking about creating excellence in other areas in a balanced way. This is paramount if we want success in all aspects of our practice and life. You will find there is a direct relationship between creating a balanced and harmonious lifestyle and your imperturbability in daily life.

CHAPTER: 20

Three Stages of Learning Explained Through Isis, Seth & Osiris

Three Stages of Any Learning Process

This chapter addresses the three phases you will experience when you undertake any great challenge, or indeed any form of training which includes a transformation of yourself.

These phases will be explained through the ancient Egyptian gods - Isis, Seth and Osiris, due to their relationship to death and rebirth.

The First Phase - Isis

This first phase is experienced when a new project is undertaken and this is considered to be attributed to that of Isis. In everyday language we would call this the honeymoon period.

In the beginnings of a new project, often you will experience this as a time of great joy and find it extremely easy to practice with little to no resistance. During this phase, there is a process of exciting discovery and a feeling of being full of energetic enthusiasm. It can almost become infatuation as you read about it, tell all your friends about it, and find yourself yearning to practice. This is a joyful and wonderful time.

But how long will this last?

Much of that depends on your own individual personality, the task you are undertaking, or skill you are developing. Some schools of learning have a very steep learning curve and in those cases the whole experience from the very beginning is extremely tough, with no form of positive feedback. In situations like that, the Isis phase can be nearly non-existent, other than just at the very start. Due to their nature and personality, some people find they spend almost the entire period in this Isis phase, and it is only right at the end that they move on to the next one. Others maybe less fortunate and find themselves moving through this rather rapidly.

The Second Phase - Seth

In the ancient Egyptian myths Seth corresponds to death. In relation to the learning process the death felt is that of the connection with the new project, in this case this is a sense of death which is caused by one's own inability to keep up with and adapt, or input the energy required to gain the skill. In reality, death is a form of transformation, not an ending. During this phase you will find aspects of your personality, indeed the very aspects that need to adapt, will try to prevent you from carrying on this course of action. You may find yourself feeling that this is impossible to master or to achieve, and you feel like you want to give up. You may find your mind offering various excuses to justify why you do not wish to continue, such as not having enough time etc.

Whatever the reasons are, they will try and draw you away from having to make the changes which are needed to achieve your goals. Some people do not realise this phase exists, so when it happens, it makes them feel like they are a failure, they feel it is the end of the goal and nothing will manifest. They spend their whole life working towards different goals, however when they get to a phase which really requires a lot effort, or where they really need to apply a new strategy, they give up and seek something new. To stop this cycle may require a change in their emotional attitude towards challenge and difficulty. This will then enable them to achieve what is necessary so they do not give up.

Trying to guide someone, or yourself, through this Seth stage can be a challenge, especially if they have never completed it and made it through to the third stage. Due to the challenging nature of this phase, often people will feel that there is no end to it and there is a feeling of wanting to give up due to the difficulty of a seemingly never ending darkness. When faced with this it is important to develop the correct attitude to help in dealing with these challenges. It is of paramount importance to keep stable and to not let the emotions take control; to continue working in a steady and calm way towards the goal. Finally, do not stop.

This process can be likened to the analogy of a new life, which grows in the darkness of the womb. When fully understood we begin to see that the darkness we are experiencing isn't that of a grave, but a place of birth not yet made manifest.

The Third Phase - Osiris

Moving on from the challenges faced in the Seth stage, you enter into the beautiful stage of Osiris. This is a time when the lessons you have learned, together with the enthusiasm from the Isis phase, begin to merge.

This combination of a new level of competency with this sense of joy brings about the wonderful outcome you have been waiting for. You have gained both the ability to guide your actions competently to make what you want happen, along with energetic enthusiasm. This new found ability gives you the chance to enjoy the fruits of your labour. The Osiris phase is where you actually get to play a bit, because with the new understanding you have gained, you are no longer practicing, you are now doing and so you can thrive.

But wait, there is another payoff for your patience and hardwork.

Having persevered through the difficult stages leading up to this, you will find that your personality has transcended its previous limitations. This will bring about beautiful changes to other aspects of your life, beyond what you could have originally dreamt of.

Let us use the analogy of a seed to view these three stages in a different way. In the first stage of the seed's journey it falls from the tree. Maybe surrounded by a beautiful fruit, it gets picked up or eaten and travels far away. The world suddenly seems full of such potential during this Isis stage. However, following on from this the world seems to take a sudden turn for the worse as the little seed finds itself trapped underground and surrounded by the dark earth. During the Seth stage it is working hard and transforming, having to pull on its reserves for seemingly little reward.

However, when it finally shoots out of the ground it is reborn, it has reached the Osiris stage.

Knowing that there is going to be a birth, a death and a rebirth in any serious undertaking can help keep us on track during that difficult Seth stage. But, it also means that we can use this road map to give us great instructions for how to make the most of each step along the learning process.

Advice on How to Gain the Most From Each Stage

During the Isis phase make sure you are fastidious in laying down your foundation. Use the momentum this stage gives to get your basic skills down, and do not let that excitement push you into rushing to the next step too quickly. Make sure during this phase you train with great circumspection, you look around and ensure you get a very broad understanding of what you are trying to do. Really utilize that initial enthusiasm in this phase to gain as much stability and routine as you can in your practice.

The Seth stage (the tough phase of death) is characterised by continual objections, so try to turn whatever the objection is around. Rather than allowing it to become a barrier, use it to power your action. So, if your mind tries convincing you

124

the action is too simplistic and beneath you, remind yourself that if it really is so easy then surely it would be no more than a triviality? Let us do it then, let us display this great competency. If on the other hand you find yourself believing that your goal is impossible and beyond your capabilities, instead practice imagining how impressive it will be when you achieve such a difficult goal. You can imagine yourself or others as watcher, whoever is important to you. Sometimes thoughts such as these are a result of those around us trying to push us down and you can turn this negativity into drive to prove them wrong. Whatever your mind uses as an objection, turn it around on itself and use that to motivate you to make it happen.

During the Osiris phase take the time to really enjoy this new competency and build high. This is a period to perfect your skill and to apply the understanding you have gained in this area. Make the most of your hard work and let the new skills you have amplify throughout the whole of your life. Rather than constraining yourself to just the new activity, take time to contemplate how much is transferrable. For example, if you have been learning the tea ceremony, then use the great degree of fastidiousness you have cultivated and use it in other areas of your life, such as cooking

125

and conversation. If you have gained great strength from body building, then take that strength and character into your personality and into your emotional life.

These are the three phases you will encounter again and again, whenever you take up great any challenge or training in your life. Now you know of them, learn to master them and you will find yourself a great student of life.

CHAPTER: 21

Mastering the Moment Before

Mastering the moment before is the secret to success. It is about preparing for the moment and creating the correct environment for the desired outcome to manifest the way we want it to.

Whenever you are about to do something, whether it is a mundane activity or a more challenging undertaking, run through a rehearsal in your mind's eye. Whilst doing this take the time to really imagine the whole process and each step leading to success. This is a natural mechanism and something which enables us to plan for the moment when we take action. The further away our task is, the more time we have to focus on creating, imagining and planning our goals. How we rehearse this in our mind's eye is very important, since it will have an affect on our actions, attitude and, as a result, outcome.

Next time you see a top sportsman or someone who is an expert at something, whether it is a skilled artist or craftsman, watch them just before they perform their art. If you look carefully you will notice there is usually point where they pause just before they begin. Often this has developed subconsciously, without the person realising it, and they are not fully aware of what really happens in this moment. So if you speak to them about this process, it brings to their attention an important skill set that they have developed.

This routine may vary slightly, but the basic elements remain the same - they clear their mind and picture success, their breathing slows, and they focus solely on their goal. Then they execute it.

Their reaction afterwards also shows a difference in expectation. Unlike many people who are pleasantly surprised when they achieve something, the assumption that they will succeed causes surprise if they don't.

So, how can you train your mind to emulate this?

In fact the answer is that you already know how to, you've just forgotten. Strangely enough, the beginner and the expert are similar in this way, hence 'beginner's luck'. When someone is shown a new task, often they have not had time to formulate resistance to success, either from others' opinions or from their own inner voice. So without the preconception of failure, they try and it works well. This beginner's luck has nothing to do with good fortune, but is actually because their newness to the task has meant they have concentrated on the steps they need to follow, and they have imagined themselves doing it well. Unfortunately, beginner's luck is often short lived, but not for the reasons you may have previously thought.

Next time you are around someone trying something new and doing well, observe the reactions of those around them to their success. You will notice that rather than reinforcing the behaviour that has produced a positive outcome, the reaction is often negative. It is extremely rare for someone to offer an encouraging response, to praise talent and immediate success in a new skill. Most people will try to convince the person it is a lot harder than it seems at this moment. Very quickly they are told that their new found ability is nothing to do with their own skill or talent, but instead the idea of beginner's luck is reinforced, robbing the person of their success and disempowering them. The seed of doubt has thus been planted.

If the person listens to this programmed response, it very often triggers the progression from the Isis to Seth stage (see previous chapter for more detail), bringing about an end to the seemingly effortless and joyful exploration that comes with at the beginning of a new endeavour. Having been told what a struggle this new skill really is, they may begin to develop a perception that the task is indeed difficult, and now view doing it as a chore.

The first step in shifting our thought patterns back to a more productive tendency is to analyse them. It is necessary to pay attention to how we visualise things; which sense we use and the feel/emotion. Some people find speaking out their thoughts are beneficial. However, it is important to listen to the inner voice, to make sure there is an uplifting, positive tone. For example, some people have an internal conversation with themselves before doing something, but if you listen carefully you will hear that the words betray a lack of confidence or the tone is negative. Others visualise the outcome of an action, and again we need to ensure this is in a positive way, rather than reinforcing negative projections.

Here are some of questions you may want to ask yourself regarding your inner voice and visualisations:

1. Is it positive in both tone and content?

2. Does it sound like someone who believes in you? (If not is this a reflection of someone in your past who maybe did not?)

3. In your imaginings are you pictured as competent?

4. Does it feel right?

5. Does it feel like it is going to work?

To achieve success we need to emulate successful thinking. Be aware this is not about deluding ourselves, we want to keep a balanced and correct assessment throughout. Rather we want to correct our visualisation of outcomes to what is realistically possible and we know we are capable of to ensure success. As this habit grows it is a really good way to develop yourself in everyday life.

For a more indepth discussion on this see the chapter 'Harmonising Disruptive Thoughts'.

CHAPTER: 22

Cultivating Positive Friendships

This chapter is about how to make the right friends; to only allow people into your life who will have a positive effect on you, and you on them. The key to this is really exciting, it allows you to make sure that instead of being trapped in cycles which are unproductive you cultivate a friendship circle with people who are uplifting.

You may have friends with whom you repeatedly go through the same negative cycles with. It is sometimes difficult to see how this friendship has developed, but the truth is you can usually map out the type of friendship you will have from the start.

When people first meet, a subconscious agreement is made as to what the relationship is going to be. It is quite hard to see this initially, but careful observation shows that in the early stages of setting up a new friendship, we present who we are and what we have to offer to the other party. Albeit in such a subtle way even we are often unaware we are doing it.

So let us imagine that on examining friendships in the past that have failed, you notice a pattern. That the people you are getting close to are often after help and a high level of involvement, but when you look back you realise that they were never interested in really solving their own problems. This type of friendship usually runs its course until you either realise they were never going to help themselves, or, more likely, you run out of the energy to continue to support their demands. Either way, their interpretation is that you rejected them and the friendship collapses.

If you then thought back to when you first met that person, and the conversations you had with them, more than likely you would find that they told you this was a repetitive cycle of their life. Of course they would have phrased it differently. Perhaps they told you how hard life is for them, how everyone around them keeps turning out to be flaky and letting them down. And when they implored you to help them, you replied.

People who do not feel a need to help in this way or get involved in this kind of friendship, would respond in a way that created distance. Perhaps they would immediately discern the person is blaming everyone else around them and know that they should take responsibility for their own life. Caution is needed before offering help.

People who do become involved in this kind of repetitive, negative cycle fail to see this. Part of the reason for this is because they are also stuck in a negative cycle whereby they are in need of attention. So being friends with this person also fulfills their own need. This co-dependent relationship creates an unhealthy friendship.

Of course, maybe they are asking for help and really do want help, but they are just too stuck in a negative cycle to be able to make the necessary changes themselves. In this situation you need to determine whether they are really willing to make the changes by giving them small tasks to lead them out of the situation. It is important that these focus on them putting in the effort. This will show the truth.

Start to look around you and you will also see other instances of negative relationships, usually with a victim and an abuser. This isn't always the way round you may expect or that first appears. On some level they will identify with each other, although it may not be conscious.

But, how can we break this pattern? How do we see what is really being presented, and what the true exchange is?

I am not special.

This is the most important idea to grasp and understand in order to break the cycle. Whenever you enter a new relationship, whether it be a job, friendship or romance, observe what is being said about those who fulfilled your role in the past and how they are now being treated. Be aware that you are no different to how they were viewed once and this will tell you more about how your relationship will develop than anything else.

So, when you get a job, look at how the boss treats their employees and know that is probably how they will treat you. When your new boyfriend or girlfriend is talking badly about their ex, remember that at one time they also said sweet words. Be aware that in the future that could be how they treat you. If you have that friend who is always gossiping or talking badly to you about a mutual friend, remember they are probably doing the same about you behind your back. When you are about to make a business deal with a new contact, listen to what they say. Are they telling you how great it is to find someone trustworthy like you, unlike everyone else they have dealt with? Are they citing stories about their terrible past experiences where they have fallen out with many people? It is important to look at this objectively.

Notice that they are the consistent element in the situations they describe; it is not possible for them to always be the victim. Beware, you are about to sign up to some trouble. Let's take the example of the businessman. Whatever the cause, by observing this interaction we can ascertain that the way they are doing business is not good. For this to be such a repetitive cycle, the reality is not that the world is against them, more likely it is related to the way they are conducting business. Perhaps it is in the way they complete deals or agreements - they may not be firm or clear enough, or maybe the goal posts get changed. Whatever it is, something is clearly not functioning as it should.

So, do not assume that you are different, or that you will be excluded from the cycle that is being told to you. Instead listen for positive messages that express how this new relationship is likely to have an uplifting effect on your life. However, if the cycle told is of constant negative characters and terrible things, be very, very cautious.

The more you look at this, the more you realise how honest people are. It is very rare for someone to imply their life is all great and for you to come join them without any hint of trouble, and for you to later on find that it is all chaos and pain.

But, you need to learn to listen. To really listen to what they are actually telling you.

If you find it difficult to see clearly because of your own trappings (especially in the beginning) you can use the reactions of those around you to help calibrate yourself. Observe how others respond, and if you find yourself out of line with everyone else, ask why. Be cautious as this approach is not foolproof, especially in a competitive environment.

A situation may occur where you find yourself repeatedly getting caught up in love triangles, or something of that nature. You will probably have a blind spot as to why this keeps occurring. Maybe someone tells you they want to be 'friends', but it is clear to everyone else they are looking for something more. Someone who is very clear on such matters would be able look at the whole scene and clearly see this. They would also see by your past interactions that this is a pattern with you and could lead to trouble. It would take a lot for the person who is caught in this cycle to be able see these things and not to continue to repeat it.

It is also worth remembering your own part in this cycle. If this is you, then look to see how you respond to other people in similar circumstances. Listen to what they say, you will find there is a strange part of you which may resonate with it, because you are used to playing this game. It can be surprisingly stubborn, refusing to hear that message. If someone advises you, 'Stay away from that person because they are trouble,' or if they say, 'It is not going to work with that person,' and you find yourself very quickly dismissing them, you need to ask yourself why.

To see through this layer of confusion it is important to understand that these confused relationship interactions are fulfilling you emotionally in some way. You feel a lacking in your life, but are not conscious aware of it.

Returning to our example earlier, if someone is always wanting to help other people, but it never seems to work out, this is because they choose people who don't want to help themselves. At first this may seem self-defeating, as they always feel let down by others. However, they also gain a sense of being in control, of being admired and of being good by trying to help someone, so they are also gaining something. Talking to them they will tell you their story, of how they try to help everyone, but people continue to throw it back in their face.

So, as you can see, identifying the cycle is only one half to solving it. To truly get out of this trap you need to identify your own internal imbalance and seek to address that. Often there are mixed intentions which cloud our actions. So if you want to help someone, truly help them. Instead of carrying out actions that create a dependency on you, seek to keep moving them towards a goal of independent success. This often requires a trail of breadcrumbs - lots of small steps by them rather than one, big, impressive finale, which is less emotionally rewarding for you, but is of the most benefit to them. If you want lots of attention, cultivate this in positive ways to help those around you, rather than getting caught up in gossip and drama. Should you wish to have an influence on your circle, rather than seeking this through manipulation and power games, look to set an example all would like to follow.

In conclusion, your emotions are seeking the kind of fulfilment that will blind you to the very message you need to hear to avoid the negative cycles in your life. Most people around you, those people who are not easily caught in that kind of situation, will see it far clearer. Once you have identified the emotional need which is out of balance, you will be able to eliminate the blind spots that are causing disharmony and begin cultivating lots of positive interactions.

CHAPTER: 23
Sometimes Seeds Do Not Grow

Sometimes when we plant a seed and do everything possible to help it grow, no matter how skilled we are, the seed fails to germinate. We can have the perfect soil, put the seed in the perfect pot, make sure it has the right drainage, position it in the right environment, with the right temperature and sunlight, water it every day and even then, sometimes that seed just does not grow.

There are times in life like this, where we do everything we possibly can to create the right circumstances for growth, but despite this we are unsuccessful. This is often when there are other variables involved, such as people or circumstances, which are out of our control. For example, if you have an argument with someone and wish to make up with them, you can do everything possible to create a nice environment for reconciliation. You can be flexible and humble in your approach, forgiving, and kind. You can say everything with the greatest of intentions to cause healing between you and even then, still sometimes the seed does not grow.

It is interesting to note that in these circumstances, when it involves other people, we tend to be less forgiving towards ourselves. Even when we have tried everything possible to do the right thing, we still believe there is a course of action we could have taken to lead to a better outcome. Still we blame ourselves, believing that we did something wrong. Yet, if we were advising a friend we would probably see the truth and reassure them that if they have done all they can, then it is up to the other person, there is no more they can do.

In my experience, the best approach to these situations, is to view them in terms of creating the environment that leads to the best possible chance for a good outcome. You want to create an opportunity for what you are trying to do to blossom, rather than thinking in terms of absolutes. So it is of benefit to focus less on the outcome (I will make this happen; if I don't, I am a bad person), and more on the attempt (I will do everything I can to reconcile). If you do this, you actually find yourself focusing on creating the environment for success more skilfully without being held back by negative emotions, or the expectation that you can control everything in the situation. This also ensures that you keep your intention true and so your actions.

CHAPTER: 24
How to Enjoy More of Your Life

No matter who you are, the circumstances of your life, or where you are in the world, there are certain tasks that you have to do each and every day. Of course, some of these tasks are more enjoyable than others. But what if it is possible to find joy in each and every thought, word, and action?

The important key to obtaining this state, is to understand that much of our enjoyment is circumstantial. It is more dependent on how we interpret the situation around us than we may at first realise. For instance, someone somewhere is in a classroom sitting detention and having to write out lines as a form of punishment. They are hating every moment of it. After they have completed the page they take it to the teacher, who looks at the lines before declaring they are not neat enough and sends them back to their desk to do it again. They feel very hurt and do not enjoy having to repeat this action. Yet, somewhere else another person is paying for a calligraphy class, whereby they are beautifully creating letters. They, on the other hand, are enjoying every moment of that class. As they form each letter, they love the adjustments and improvements suggested to them. Like before, they take the completed sheet to their teacher, who upon seeing the work instructs them to repeat it. And they do so, loving the meditative nature of this continual improvement.

You may be able to see this interesting phenomena in your own life as well. If you know someone who is really into physical fitness, maybe they do crossfit or go to the gym regularly, you will most likely see a difference in attitude towards physical exertion dependent on the context. If you phone them to suggest meeting up and doing some great functional training together, they will most likely eagerly accept. Replace that with building work or clearing land (similar output required), and you are less likely to get such a positive response to your invitation. Although the same physical exertion would be required for doing either activity, the reaction to the latter may be viewed in a more negative way, due to being perceived as less fun; one activity is viewed as play and the other as work. So the key is to find enjoyment in that activity and gain the most from it, to understand perception is just in our mind.

This distinction between work and play is often instilled into us as children at school. During these formative years the day is split between lessons and play, with play very much being treated as the reward of work. This is often reinforced at home with parents insisting children complete homework before playing. If you watch a young child before this has been drummed into them, you will see they are as interested in housework as they are in play, wanting to join in with all activities without prejudice. This is before they have learnt which ones they should enjoy and which they should find tedious. This is what we must learn to recapture.

In order to unlock the key to our full potential, it is important to fully engage with each and every activity. Not just with the mind, but the heart and body too. This may sound strange to begin with, but by engaging all of yourself you will find that you become both more efficient and enjoy the task more. This makes the process more rewarding, which in turn is encouraging and will lead to less resistance next time you need to carry out the task.

So, to engage these three areas we can follow this method:

Firstly, it is necessary to engage the body; by sitting up straight we let ourselves know it is time to focus. Conversely, if you are doing a task that stresses you out, try to adopt a more relaxed position.

Secondly, we need to create an environment that is conducive to work in, which makes it easier to engage our mind. For example, if you are completing paperwork, try to make sure you are undisturbed and working in a room that is quiet, so you can concentrate.

Thirdly, we engage our heart (emotions). To do this you need to know your own heart and what you value in life. Once you understand what you desire, you can use this to motivate yourself to stay on target and to excel.

So, if self-improvement is something you enjoy, aim to develop your skill each time you carry out your task. When you are driving your car to work in the morning, see it as practicing coordination, reactions, and patience. Need to take a different route? This is a chance to practice memorisation. Perhaps you are having a conversation with someone, but find the subject boring? This can become concentration training. Find the value in each situation.

This can become an enjoyable experience and tasks that you once dreaded can even start to be the ones you look forward to. You need to find what it is that motivates you and, once you incorporate it in all you do, you will find a noticeable change to how you face challenges in life.

Many people find boredom difficult to deal with. If there are circumstances where there is an unavoidable wait, we can either utilise that time positively, or use it as a form of patience training. Within the Zen tradition mundane work is used as a form of awareness training. In other traditions, such as *Bhakti* yoga, the intention is to perform every task with an act of love. This sense of love for all living creatures is expressed through doing everything to the best standard possible.

When you start to view all challenges with this new outlook, then the world takes on an entirely different colour and light. You will find this beautiful harmonising process starts to become external as well. You start to harmonise with the world and with everything that is happening.

CHAPTER: 25
Make an Appointment With Happiness

I have found the most powerful results have come from the most simple of things. I would like to talk to you about a technique that is uplifting and helps you get into the ideal state of mind that will allow you to thrive and enjoy life. I am talking about booking an appointment with happiness. This may seem like a very strange concept, but it is actually something we tend to do naturally.

If you think back to your childhood you can probably remember a time where there was a great television show you really enjoyed that came on every week, or an opportunity to go to class or see a friend who was an inspiration to us. Something you really built up and looked forward to. Somehow, it seemed to make the time in between far easier to deal with. Even now when reflecting back on it, you may feel a sense of joy.

Sometimes in adult life this kind of thing can get crowded away. I believe booking that appointment with happiness can have a bigger impact than medication for some people. I recommend that you book two or three of these a week. Perhaps one with a person, or a group of people, who are in tune with you and encourage you to bring out your good qualities. Another one I would suggest should be an activity. This could be something that involves practicing good posture, either of the body (such as yoga) or the mind (such as painting). These appointments don't have to be anything big, sometimes a program we enjoy, learning a new skill, or reading a book can ensure that we make time for ourselves and create balance.

You will find people who are natural masters of this art have a way to make moments out of time. They have specific rituals and routines to savour each moment - a seat they sit in to read their favourite book, or a little treat while watching their favourite sport. This is really powerful because savouring that moment creates a ripple, a change in a state of consciousness that amplifies throughout your week. So there it is, book an appointment (or two, or three) with happiness every week. Put it in the diary and remember this is an important part of your emotional and mental wellbeing.

CHAPTER: 26

A Spiritual Person's Guide to Making Money

This teaching is for those who wish to make money to have a better effect on the world around them. This will help them to improve the lives of the ones they love, help those in need and to be able to escape the nine to five so they can fully enjoy and explore life.

First, is is necessary to observe and understand the financial system which we live under. Then we will examine the methods used by those just after money and why we should not imitate them. Finally, how we can apply spiritual principles in order to gain wealth through genuine expression and improvement of who we are and what we want to do in the world.

When we think about money, we think about notes and coins. You have probably noticed that the currency we use features images of powerful authority figures such as presidents, royalty, and famous figures who have made a significant contribution to society, such as inventors. There are also other symbols of authority, such as coats of arms. This is because money is the physical representation of power, it is how the human race has divided power and how it is controlled.

If you look at the animal kingdom you will observe that some animals make noises at one another, such as barking or chirping. This is how they decide who is in charge, quite simply the loudest animal gains dominance. This barking can escalate into violence, more so with some species than others. Some instead compete using athletic displays, showing off plumage, or marking their territory in some way. All of these displays have the same aim, to intimidate the opponent into submission.

Humans do all of those things to some degree, but as society has evolved we as a race have changed them to appear more 'civilised' and developed an easy to display marker for status - money. This is what our whole community and the system we live in is based on. So although it may seem as though we have risen above our animal instincts, the truth is we've just transformed them into something distinctly human.

In order to make sure we keep working, the system has been designed with strategies to make it almost impossible for us to function without it. If you don't have much money then you must work hard to make it and then spend most of it on paying a landlord for shelter, to buy food and clothing. If you do manage to gain enough to buy your own house, the world is set up in such a way that you are most likely now tied into paying a mortgage for many years and, should you stumble, you will find yourself back at the bottom working your way up. The world is set up in such a way that we are convinced to not take responsibility for our own environment, so instead of dealing with our waste we delegate and pay for someone else to. This of course means we have to work even harder. Yet, if you look at the truly rich you will notice a difference. They already have money (power), so they can invest that money instead of working in the same way as you and I. Because they are contributing what in our society is seen as most important (money), they are rewarded the most for the hard work of those below them. Even if you start to work your way up the rungs of your chosen career, you will find that there are procedures in place to stop you making it too far.

It is quite evident that the system is designed to keep everyone in a constant cycle of work. Likewise, there are some clever taxes in place to stop those who do well from helping others to step up too. This is because the system only works if the majority are on the bottom. Taxes such as those applied to gifts and inheritance stop this upwards mechanism. To truly understand the full extent of this system, we must start from the beginning.

From the moment you were born, you were part of a system that is designed to make you a good worker. The schooling system starts you gently with a few mornings or afternoons, this extends until you are in school five days a week. You are then given homework, which extends this day for you, albeit at home. By the time you leave school you are used to the majority of the day being spent at work. There is another important lesson taught at school too - to pay attention to authority. You are discouraged from breaking the mould and expected to follow the timetable with everyone else. Even your learning is expected to fit a timetable, and there is concern should a target not be met when expected.

In your adult life there are similar expectations. Should you try to change that, even with good reason, you will soon feel resistance, as those with the power/money want anything that breaks that system to be stopped. We need to look at this and we need to enjoy the fact we are a part of this big monopoly game. However, we also need to understand what a big challenge this is. There are very few people who manage to get free, most spend the majority of their lives doing work they don't like just to get by, not thriving.

So to understand we need to look at two types of people; those who look just to make money and those who are wealthy in both financial and personal terms.

Of those who are in the first category, making money is their main motive in life, and their job tends to reflect this, since they are not trying to balance a good family life or emotional fulfilment. Perhaps they have decided to go into real estate, become a lawyer, or set up a business. They tend to work in environments that would burn others out, but for them they are simply focused on making as much money as possible and then usually converting this into other symbols of power/success - fast cars, expensive suits, big houses.

Of course, there are many who have this goal, but don't succeed, and even those that do, often feel that what they have isn't enough. So they put in more effort. Unfortunately their efficiency tends to go down, so the people I have witnessed who are very successful businessmen always seem tired and lack energy outside of work. And the sacrifice they have made is often large. So hard have they worked to get the money, they are now too tired and without the time to enjoy it.

This obsession with making money also tends to be addictive, so what happens is the more money they make, the more they spend, and the more things they want. It's not uncommon for those on a large wage to have a big mortgage and credit card debts. Even worse, their focus on making money has made them blind to the importance of other things in life, so often it is very difficult for them to keep relationships. They never see their wife or husband much, which leads to divorce and they end up with a very big house, but not very happy. They tend to become completely taken in by the system and they actually start to believe that the value of someone is how much money they make. If you talk to them reflecting on their life, often their regrets are not having spent enough time with those they love or actually taking time to enjoy the world.

The danger of focusing on money is that the elemental imbalance within can take over and you can start to become corrupted by it, obsessed by its accumulation. That is not to say that everyone becomes like this, but it is a risk you take.

It may happen in a way you least expect. For example, someone who is sensitive and thoughtful may want to be free. They want to be free in the sense that they do not want to need a job, to keep working day in and day out. To them this seems like it would be a wasted life. It's this fear that traps them. They are fearful that they will have to work forever in drudgery, so they take on many side projects looking for a way out, a way to make enough money they no longer need to worry. Their sensitivity means they are hurt by things others may seem as trivial, but they are looking for a job that has no toughness or hardship to it, yet pays enough to be secure. So it is they go in endless cycles, working twice as hard in search of this ultimate job. Their goal has become to make money. If instead they could accept the inherent difficulties all of life has in some way, then instead of spending their spare time chasing other work, they could use it to enjoy elements of life they want to be free to enjoy in the first place.

If your heart is led by money rather than genuine reasons the work itself becomes harder and more tedious. It is hard because with no other motive than money, you need to constantly adjust your attitude to keep going. Much of the advice given to entrepreneurs and businessmen is mimicking behaviour that should come naturally if you are doing something for genuine reasons.

They will tell you to always:

1. Smile to your customers

2. Make sure you communicate with them often

3. Ensure you have the right attitude toward them

4. Take up networking opportunities and make lots of friends.

They will give you the kinds of adjustments which are natural when your heart is in it and tell you things that anyone doing something they enjoy does not need to know.

But, how do we do it? How do we win the right way?

We do not want to become corrupted by money, we do not want to become obsessed by it, we do not want to sacrifice our life for it. So, how do we do it?

Well, we need to rise above it in the sense we need to focus on something bigger than money.

For this reason, it is far better to focus on the goal, and rather view money as the means to reach it. You may find you need to keep correcting your mind to ensure you don't get taken off track.

There are some people in life who deliberately choose a path that means they can enjoy what they love to do while still earning enough money to live and spend time with their family. An example of this is someone I knew who was an artist. He deliberately chose a day job that was not that challenging or really stressful, but paid enough for him and his family to live comfortably. This then enabled him to do his job well, but when at home still be alert and have enough energy to paint and spend time with his family. He managed to enjoy his life without sacrificing any of the things he valued.

Unfortunately he died very early, and at his funeral his work colleagues were unable to see the value in his life. They did not praise him for the fact he was always fun, or for his talent as an artist, or for the way he was such a good father. But instead pitied him, for they felt that he had not reached his potential financially. They felt he had held back and he should have instead been making more money, which they considered a higher priority. But these people were so trapped that they were unable to see that what he achieved was far greater than any price tag.

So the mission is summarised as follows: If you can't find a job that gives you the space you need to do what you want, find a job that is what you want.

Find a Way to Be Paid To Play

So we have spoken about working in such a way as to leave space for you to spend time on what you value, but what if you can make what you value your work? Find a way to be paid for what you enjoy doing and, for many people, this is the key. If you can find this, everything else will fall into place. However, the steps may be small and to begin with do not think in terms of how to make big money. Instead think in terms of having enough to get by, and over time everything else will fall into place.

For various reasons you may not be able to change jobs. In fact, you may find that rather than changing what you are doing, you just need to find what it is you enjoy about your current job. However, if you are in a job you truly hate, this is unlikely to have a positive effect.

So what happens once you are doing something that you genuinely love and you feel is valuable in the world? Well, you create a receptacle for your positivity and those teachings you have learned, such as the Law of Attraction, become far easier to put into practice when you are doing something you truly believe in. Positive thought can go a long way, but it is difficult to think positively when your actions are simply a means to an end. When you are genuinely inspired, your enthusiasm will be infectious and unstoppable. It will be difficult for those around you to not want to join you and in this way success will grow. It is better to start off poor and be a yoga teacher than be a wealthy accountant if you love yoga, but hate accounts.

It is difficult to make that first leap of faith, but remember all you need is enough to get by, just enough. Then a wonderful thing happens, you may be doing more, but the extra effort you need to put in disappears because you are enjoying what you are doing. In fact you have a hard time stopping because you are enjoying it so much. You will also find yourself naturally working smarter rather than harder. This is because you are more motivated and so stay on target easier; what would take you half an hour with distractions and constant refocus, now takes no longer than ten minutes. On top of this, you will find your life naturally balances out, which means you are resting properly and there is time for you practice those things that are important to you, such as your spiritual path.

This balancing effect goes full circle and has a positive effect on your work. You are resting better, so your productivity increases; this means you have more time for your spiritual exercises, so you you are evolving your consciousness and becoming more aware and more skillful; as you become more aware you find it easier to be in tune with the world around you and are on target more. Everything you do continually improves and becomes more and more effective. Your input now yields far greater results across your life. You start to work smart not hard, and the financial success is a side effect of this.

Think back to your own life and you may recognise a time when life seemed to just flow and was accompanied by effortless success. From personal experience this has been most obvious through book writing. When the motivation is genuinely from the heart, I have always found that the success is far greater than when I have been motivated by commercial reason. No matter how well targeted a book seems, when the motivation behind writing it is to create an income the opposite has occurred and the book has not sold as well as expected. However, when a project is undertaken with passion and enthusiasm this transfers and others enjoy the book too. Even when the book is being written, in the first case it is far harder and requires a lot more effort.

This is similar to someone trying to fall in love. They can go through all the right motions and struggle to say the right words, but when it is not genuine it feels like hard work. Yet, to the couple who are head over heels in love, nothing seems too much, poetry falls from their lips and everything flows naturally.

As always, we need to be aware of the Hermetic principle 'as above, so below'. When everything in you is motivated and onboard, you will find external forces lend their aid too. If instead you are working against your nature, how can you expect others around you to support your venture?

This path will lead to enlightenment at work. Your job should be another means of self-development and in this way you will start to rise through merit. Your reputation will start to improve because you are excellent, because you are genuinely wonderful at what you are doing and this cannot be hidden. Your genuine enthusiasm for your work will naturally guide you to do all the things that other people tell you to do to make money. So networking will be replaced by making friends, recruiting will be replaced by finding allies, and you will not need to create a positive mental outlook because you will have one. Every single thought, word and action towards your business will have ripples that will bring back success.

And most of all your attitude towards money will change. So money may be power to society at large, but to you it will be the ability to do good. Instead you will think in terms of the wonderful things you can do with it. If you want to go on holiday, aim for the holiday; if you want to help someone who is in need, think of them; if you want to buy something, go somewhere, or do something that is good, that has a good effect on those you love, imagine the smiles on their faces rather than looking for zeros on your paycheck.

In conclusion, the aim is to put yourself in a position to do the things you love to do. Focus on what you want to achieve, focus on what light you want to spread, what good you want to do, what fun you want to have and let the money be a side effect that shows when you are getting it right.

CHAPTER: 27
Contemplation of Oneness

I would like you to join me in a contemplation exploring the concept of oneness. To do this I would like you to imagine certain scenes. These scenes explore the interconnected whole, and the natural network found between things.

The first scene I would like you to picture in your mind's eye is that of the sea. Imagine before you a vast ocean, take a moment to really picture it. 'Sea' refers to the expanse of water, yet we have other words for different aspects of this picture you have imagined. Perhaps you can see the movement of the current, or there are waves, or even spray? Let us contemplate the concept of a wave. A wave starts as simply part of the sea, but part of the sea then forms and becomes the wave, yet we would not say it had stopped being the sea. After a moment it splashes down, once again becoming simply sea. So, a wave is a separate part of a whole that it is never removed from. And indeed if we artificially removed it, it would no longer be a wave nor the sea. So the idea of a separate aspect of a bigger picture, that is both dependent on the whole for identity and yet separate, is already within the bounds of our understanding.

I would like you to move your attention now to a different scene. Imagine a blood cell going around your body. I want you to imagine this blood cell is special in the sense it that it has become self-aware. So let us really use our imagination. This special blood cell now realises that it is alive, that to some degree it has its own nervous system, takes in nutrition, and eliminates waste. In a sense every cell in our body is indeed a being in its own respect. Returning back to our self-aware cell going around its daily business, it quite clearly has its own physical borderlines and it knows there are other cells outside of those borderlines it can influence, but cannot directly control. It has got its own life, it knows it was born out of other cells and that it will die as other cells do. It would be a very confusing and unrealistic idea to try to explain to that cell it is actually part of a great being which has got a higher consciousness. Now that special cell would understandably be in disbelief and if it was then told that its entire purpose to life was to keep the whole going, it may feel a little confused or uncertain. You could try to get the cell to understand, maybe by getting it to imagine amplifying its awareness. But to that cell, this would seem like a far out and unrealistic idea. But, if it was able to grasp this maybe it could sense something, feel some of the patterns and signals in the body. Perhaps it could even begin to see an underlying pattern in what was going on, a purpose to all the apparently random events going on around it.

Now let us imagine another scene in nature. There is a remote island with fruit trees, photosynthesising and taking nutrition through the roots. As they grow they produce fruit which the birds eat. The birds then fly away having eaten them and they deposit the seeds. This is how the fruit trees are spread throughout the island. Let us imagine that on the island there is nothing else that eats the fruit from the trees except the birds, and the birds do not eat anything but the fruit from the tree. So if one dies out completely, so will the other.

We can start to see that the fruit trees and birds are more interconnected than they may first appear. Perhaps the two are even closer than we think, maybe the bird is simply an extension of the fruit tree, a movable part. Could it be that this bird is part of the tree's reproductive system? But we can switch this. Maybe the apple tree is the way for the bird to get nutrition from the sun? All the arguments we can make against the bird and the tree being one, can be used to say the cell in the body is also separate.

Let's now move to a more traditional spiritual contemplation - becoming at one with the universe. In many traditions, breaking the cycle of death and rebirth is seen as the ultimate aim, an inevitable realisation either through a special technique or process. It is thought this will expand our awareness, stop us being limited and we will become something more. Yet, if we look at the previous scenes it would be a very strange thing to start training a wave to become more of the sea, wouldn't it?

The cell does not need to do any work to be a part of our body, it already is. So, why would we need to make it struggle? What would this struggle do? What would the cell gain? Surely if it is struggling that is reinforcing this idea of separateness? Surely the idea that there is something to escape, or become, is contrary to this whole idea of oneness?

So perhaps like the bird, it is possible not to realise how interconnected we are. It does not know how reliant or at one it is with the fruit, nor indeed the tree, and, by extension, the sun and the soil. But perhaps it is just as connected as the wave is to the sea, or the cell is in the body.

As our final contemplation, we imagine that the borderlines between us are not as distinct as they may at first seem. As I write this to you now my thoughts become words on the page, and when you read them they become thoughts in your mind's eye. So whose thoughts are they?

Perhaps if we contemplate this deeply we would realise that the processes of death and rebirth cannot be escaped because it is not real. There is nothing we can do to make ourselves become at one with everything, because there is no 'becoming' - we are already there. A shift in perspective and expansion of our understanding and sense of self will reveal this to us. The immortality, the freedom is there. But like the cell, we have to let go of the sense of self associated with being a cell. We would have to let go of the idea of ourselves in order to become fully aware what we really are. Perhaps when thinking about letting go of our ego. We should not be thinking in terms of being humble or letting go of any form of pride, but we should think in terms of expanding our sense of self to encompass more and letting go of any petty small sense of who we could be.

Indeed could we imagine that maybe this whole process could involve just shifting our perspective through letting go?

CHAPTER: 28
Harmony Leads to Enlightenment

If you explore spiritual traditions around the world as I have, you soon realise that the goal of almost all paths is to achieve a sense of oneness, a unity with all things. Some paths believe the best way to achieve this is through the destruction of the ego. It has always seemed contradictory to me that traditions wanting to get rid of the ego would focus on self-development to do so. I do not think there is anything to destroy, rather I think that true unity is simply awakening to how interconnected we are. Instead, I believe a positive, outgoing and caring philosophy, where we focus on kindness and on living in harmony, will bring the results we seek.

I believe that to reach our highest potential, we need to move our focus to that of harmony. To aim to harmonise with all living things, and rather than fighting against the current, embrace everything you are and everything that is.

We have to accept that there are things that need to transform and things that we need to overcome. Look to harmonise these aspects of life and when facing challenges or undertaking a task, aim to bring it into balance, just as we do with our personality. By improving our character and transforming ourselves and the world around us, this philosophy acts like a sunlight on the soul. As time goes on our old sense of self starts to disappear and who we really are emerges. In this way a beautiful discovery awaits, that of our true nature.

ABOUT THE AUTHOR

Martin marks his spiritual training as beginning when he was five years old with martial arts. It was here he first learnt self-discipline and control, lessons which he found invaluable when his spiritual practice began during his teenage years. Although he became an accomplished martial artist, it is this quest for knowledge that became his life's true passion and dedication.

Through the perfection of the art of meditation, his mission has always been to seek out the human potential that lies within all of us and to harness it for the betterment of oneself and others.

*'My inner quest is to discover my full
potential through the art of meditation,
to use this skill to make the most of my
time on earth and have the most
beneficial effect while I am here. To
bring out the best in myself in order to
be of the best service to the world...'*

Through diligent and unbroken disciplined practice for over twenty years, he has gained the fruits of such endeavours, demonstrating skillful control over the elements and his mind. Believing that such potential should not be hidden and the knowledge available to those who seek it, this is what inspired him to begin demonstrating such abilities online.

His experience as a practitioner in this art includes extensive studies that have seen him travel around the world, searching out traditions and masters to further his knowledge on the subject. He generously shares with us the keys to success in meditation, which are also transposable into our everyday lives. To Martin,

*'meditation is the ultimate skill, the mastery of
which leads to mastery of all other skills.'*

One of his greatest achievements is that of personal development and overcoming obstacles and challenges in his own life through applying the same principles that he applies in meditation.

'Only when our knowledge of inner technologies and abilities matches our outer progress will we reach our full potential.'

Martin runs the Seshen School of Meditation, which is dedicated to the growth and self-mastery of its students.

Finally, his positivity and humility leave a lasting impression on you.

'The potential that lies in our own consciousness, if used correctly, never ceases to amaze me, and I believe that it is through this inner study we as a race can learn to live in greater harmony with our own bodies and with the world around us…Of course, the greatest lessons come from practice and, through diligent daily dedication to the art of meditation for over 20 years, I have gained what I believe is a clear vision of the full potential in us all. How the vibrations created through our meditation can become one with our daily consciousness.'

~ Martin Faulks

'*I would like you to imagine a rather strange situation. The prince has left his kingdom and lost his memory. While he has been away he has been made king, but is not aware of this. Upon returning to his palace everything seems new to him, but also feels somewhat familiar. As he walks through the palace some of the guards become aware of his confusion and seek to take advantage of it. When he asks them to open the gate to the garden or to help him with something they ask for things in return. They try to ask him to make deals with them and if he becomes frustrated or angry they know he is not aware of what is happening. Sometimes even if they do as he says they do it in a way that has a trick or a nasty edge to it. Soon some of the other servants join in and even start trying to divide the whole palace and its grounds up between them. Because they know he is the true owner they do this by trying to make deals with him, or by tricking him at every turn. Now and again he is lucky enough to meet a higher ranking and more loyal member of his staff who try their best to remind him of his true position as gently as possible. Imagine how different it would have been if he had returned fully aware and able to see how things really are. Would those members of the palace have seemed negative in any way to him then?*'

Printed in Poland
by Amazon Fulfillment
Poland Sp. z o.o., Wrocław